I ONLY
Walk
ON *Water*
WHEN IT
Rains

PATTY L. LUCKENBACH

BALBOA
PRESS

A DIVISION OF HAY HOUSE

Scripture take from The New Oxford Annotated Bible, Revised Standard Version. (1971) New York, N.Y. Oxford University Press.

Balboa Press books may be ordered through booksellers or by contacting:

Balboa Press
A Division of Hay House
1663 Liberty Drive
Bloomington, IN 47403
www.balboapress.com
1 (877) 407-4847

Because of the dynamic nature of the Internet, any web addresses or links contained in this book may have changed since publication and may no longer be valid. The views expressed in this work are solely those of the author and do not necessarily reflect the views of the publisher, and the publisher hereby disclaims any responsibility for them.

The author of this book does not dispense medical advice or prescribe the use of any technique as a form of treatment for physical, emotional, or medical problems without the advice of a physician, either directly or indirectly. The intent of the author is only to offer information of a general nature to help you in your quest for emotional and spiritual well-being. In the event you use any of the information in this book for yourself, which is your constitutional right, the author and the publisher assume no responsibility for your actions.

Any people depicted in stock imagery provided by Thinkstock are models, and such images are being used for illustrative purposes only.
Certain stock imagery © Thinkstock.

Print information available on the last page.

ISBN: 978-1-5043-5556-8 (sc)
ISBN: 978-1-5043-5558-2 (hc)
ISBN: 978-1-5043-5557-5 (e)

Library of Congress Control Number: 2016906133

Balboa Press rev. date: 05/21/2016

I dedicate this book to my grandchildren. May their hearts deliver visions of the beauty and wisdom of their rich heritage. May they have the courage to remember that the true spirit lives within them, and may they each become wise grandfathers and grandmothers. May all suffering be transformed, and may they be called carriers of grace. It is within their hands that they behold their hearts, sing the songs, light the fires, and follow the drums home. We are all related.

CONTENTS

FOREWORD

Many books are interesting and informative. Then there are those rare, special ones that go well beyond that. These books are deeply compelling, even transforming. Congratulations! You are holding a book of the latter variety—a book that is both a precious gift and a profound blessing.

It has been a tremendous privilege for me to work and serve with Dr. Patty Luckenbach for over three decades. My respect for her and her spiritual heart is immense. I haven't known very many spiritual leaders who have given as much of themselves, of their energy and caring, as has Dr. Patty. She is a tireless, enthusiastic, loving, and devoted lantern of compassion and truth. Amid her many contributions and traits, she equally exudes abundant joy and good humor.

However, there are several other qualities that are supremely important to highlight. Dr. Patty Luckenbach is a spiritual pilgrim impelled by unmistakable and steadfast courage. This courage leaps from all these pages as Dr. Patty challenges herself, stretches herself, immerses herself, and relentlessly grows herself. As you read this powerful book, the opportunities available for us all to leap into expanded dimensions of knowing and being will become obvious and inescapable. Dr. Patty's example beckons us to the endless adventure of becoming for which we are designed and destined. I imagine she would simply and directly ask each of us, "Why not now?"

Shakespeare wrote of "tongues in trees, books in running brooks, sermons in stones, and good in everything." In your journey through this book, you'll experience firsthand how Dr. Patty has fine-tuned her spiritual sensitivity so as to appreciate the caress of the divine, to receive its higher instructions, and to celebrate the spirit in everything. She has placed a welcome mat at the doorway of her heart, always inviting the sacred to enter. A hallmark of spiritual advancement is to enhance receptiveness and elevate one's "spiritual antennae" so that the subtle, ethereal aspects of reality can be discerned and explored. For Dr. Patty, all of nature is a favorite guide, a wellspring of insights, healing, and breakthroughs. Thus the material in this book offers a priceless gift, especially for a culture so enticed and driven by intellectual, material, and technological means and ends. It is the gift of reconnection with the natural world, with the earth and all its creations. Here is an incomparable wellspring from which to grow an essential antidote to much of the emptiness, depression, and lack of purpose that afflict so many.

Dr. Patty Luckenbach is a respected and beloved minister and teacher of *Science of Mind and Spirit*, or what is sometimes termed *New Thought, Ageless Wisdom.* As illustrated by the slice of her life shared in this book, she also chose to embark upon a pilgrimage into the wisdom and richness of the indigenous Native American paths, particularly the ways of the Lakota. She didn't simply sample these teachings—she feasted on them and has become an honorary member of this nation, an emissary of its wisdom and power. It is extraordinary that she has become a master of two intricate and transformative spiritual systems, allowing each to inform and enrich the other. We who walk by her side—and now you, the reader—are the beneficiaries!

Travel with Dr. Patty down the Path of the Feather, the Path of Heart, the Path of Inner Wisdom, the Path of Transformation, and the Path of Cosmic Light. Receive the inspiration and empowerment of the bear. Enter the kingdom of the mysterious and the miraculous, and be blessed. As Dr. Patty quotes Zen master teacher Thich Nhat Hahn, "The miracle is not to walk on water. The miracle is to walk on the green earth, dwelling deeply in the present moment and feeling truly alive."

Dearest Patty, I am so very grateful that you have shared your remarkable spiritual journey so generously and honestly. I have cherished our shared passages to the sacred realms within. I honor you for all you have done, and moreover for all you have become. You are a sage, a crone, and a fountain of healing heart. I am delighted that so many searchers and students will now be blessed by your deep wisdom and commitment. May you, and all of us, continue to discover feathers of confirmation that life is good, that a great path beckons, that the resources needed are already given, and that the indwelling beloved is eager to grace us with love and light.

Dance on!
With abiding love,

Dr. Roger W. Teel
Senior Minister and Spiritual Director
Mile Hi Church
Lakewood, Colorado

Dr. Patty Luckenbach recounts her life experiences and the building of relationships with the Lakota people of the Great Plains of this country. With both seriousness and humor, her story touches deeply into the spiritual truths that were revealed to her as she participated with the Lakota people in their spiritual practices and celebrations. As she learned about herself and of life's many ways, she shows us that life cannot be better until we walk with each other in peace, harmony, justice, and wisdom.

The Lakota people were gifted a pipe of peace by a spiritual being called the White Buffalo Calf Woman a few centuries ago. After the gift of the pipe, the Lakota people developed Seven Rites and some derived rituals around the use of the pipe in prayer. Dr. Patty was allowed and included in some of these rituals of prayer to celebrate the creator and creation. She learned that everything is related, as is expressed by the Lakota saying, "Mitakuwe Oyas'in." She was adopted as a sister into a Lakota family through the Lakota Hunka, the relative making and naming ritual of the Lakota Sacred Pipe. She experienced healing and the truths of the universe through the derivative rites of the Pipe. All of this revealed to her who she is and the connection all of life has in expressing Spirit in the walk of life. Many may joyfully find agreement with what is shared here. Some may not. But whatever is experienced by those who tune into this story, it is a genuine and authentic experience. Those of us who shared it with her had great fun and enjoyment in praying and celebrating with her. May she continue for a long time!

Howard P. Bad Hand

Author of *Native American Healing*

PREFACE

I Only Walk on Water When It Rains is a guide for mystical cosmic consciousness and questing for unity in the wilderness. It is wisdom through stories and conversation with the Great Bear Spirit. The stories and conversation reveal astonishing magic, mystery, miracles, and magical song. Meister Eckhart wrote, "This spirit seeks to be broken through by God." Source God, the creative love-intelligence, leads us through a desert into the wilderness and solitude of the divine where God is pure unity, where God gushes up within itself. To live in the rightful means to live within consciousness. There is a cosmic life that lies within us as a compass on our paths.

Carolyn Myss states in her book *Embracing the Castle*, "Our journey on life's path we seek to walk with generous equilibrium. Life asks us to walk with humility.... Humility is a quality of character that you must have on the spiritual path. Humility, understood within a spiritual context is the portal to complete liberation and spiritual equilibrium. Living in a state of being spiritually awake we realize that true humility is rooted in our divine awareness."[1]

May we walk in balance and realize we move in an electromagnetic field of grace. Dr. Ernest Holmes states, "All the Power there is, all the Presence there is, all the Love there is, all the Peace there is, all the Good there is, and the Only God there is, is Omnipresent."[2] It is this magnetic love that gives us our true north. We trust that the rightful is the path of heart and living within the consciousness of a greater and powerful creator, as we walk in balance. Nothing is worshipped as a single god; it's seen as a pearl upon the golden chain of divinity. Be aware as you walk your path. All paths lead back to our hearts' doors, and all of life is holy and sacred. You'll have dry leaves turn to rose petals that soften the soles of your feet. This is a guide for a cosmic journey of consciousness.

---

[1]   C. Myss, *Entering the Castle* (New York: Free Press, 2007), 110.

[2]   Dr. E. Holmes, *Science of Mind* (Los Angeles: Science of Mind Publishing, 1974), 323.

I am companioned on my path by the Great Bear Spirit, who shares humorous and profound healing wisdoms. The bear spirit represents a great creator who is powerful and walks in balance. The bear addresses the divine fibers of life and the gift of interconnection, which gives witness to the cosmic patterns. The inner forest is alive with the power of Bear. I would like to share these visions which have come to me. The visions have opened a transparent window to my heart. The visions have offered understanding of a cosmic connection.

With heartfelt respect and dignity, I share my experience of the Native Americans. I'm thankful for the soul of the American Indian. I hold respect and honor for the invitation of the relationship of the Hunka (Making of Relations) ceremony, where the White Lance family chose my husband and me as their brother and sister. The indigenous wisdom has opened my heart to a deeper feeling of a mystical communion. I'm grateful for the wisdom of all indigenous nations. I honor and bless the golden thread of wisdom which has been woven by stories and ceremonies. The healing thread of wisdom continues to reflect an interconnection that is available to all people. A powerful Native American leader, Duane Hollow Horn Bear, great grandson of the famous Chief Hollow Horn Bear, whose heart was healing from the broken arrows of racism, said, "We all have red hearts." We are all related.

ACKNOWLEDGMENTS

In gratitude to the magnificent teachers and visionary leaders who are dedicated to their spiritual paths and walk with humility and radiant love, I honor and thank: Gabe Morella; Howard Bad Hand; Homer White Lance; Albert White Hat, Sr.; Jorge Luis Delgado; Gabi Dettke-Garcia; Albert Baniyam; Dr. Roger Teel; Dr. Thomas Hora; Dr. Ernest Holmes; my husband, Luke Luckenbach; Teri Kulas; Carolyn Varvel, RScP.; Colleen Nelson, RScP.; and my most respectful friend, the bear. These blessed individuals have taught me to humbly walk on water when it rains.

INTRODUCTION

Upon my arrival on this big green earth, my mother, father, and grandparents shared a hundred times with friends and family that I was born with thick black hair, and they called me their little Indian.

My family honored my grandmother's Swedish heritage and traditions. It was amazing in my adult years that I was called the Lakota Swede by my Lakota family and friends. I earned the name Wakaygli Wasi Wingyag, "Woman Who Dances with Lightning," and I was given the name Carte Waste Wisa, "Good-hearted Woman."

I was born into a family where prayer was the life force that healed and revealed grace and mercy in the midst of suffering and pain. I have questioned life and listened with the breath of holy light to the wisdom of the ages. It was my father who took my hand and made sure I attended church the summer before his passing; he and I were baptized together. Perhaps he was telling me good-bye because he knew that I'd always walk a spiritual path. I understood not to be afraid, because I saw in my father undaunted strength and courage, and my mother reflected a strong spiritual belief in the power of prayer and love.

My mother told me how proud my grandpa would have been to know my heartfelt connection with the Lakota and medicine people throughout the world. Grandpa was a great man and had personal friends who were men of all color and walks of faith. During the week, Grandpa smelled like engine oil because he worked as a blue-collar worker for the city on heavy equipment. I always knew his hands could repair anything. He never attended church on Sundays, but he would dress up in his suit and tie and take us out to dinner. I remember the long rides in the country after a nice Sunday dinner and church with the family. On his death bed, his Indian, Jewish, Spanish, and black brothers visited him to pray in their own faiths for a good man's passage. He will always be remembered as a man of integrity, respect, humbleness, and joy.

I learned to explore country roads with Grandpa on Sunday afternoons, and I continue to explore the side roads of life. If the paths before me were paved and looked easy, I chose cutting through the forest and built a new path. I'm not sure whether it was my sun sign that I was born under, or whether it was simply the need to explore and discover new things, but my path has taken me out on a limb many times. It's been a challenge to figure out my way back to the heart of the tree and find my rootedness in the nature of being.

I learned early in life that I need to keep my sense of humor. Others often referred to me as a pioneer, and I had to walk with lightness while I was exploring. Humor is an elixir that brings forth balance and harmony. Humor acts as a stabilizer and can equalize an energy field.

After the death of my father when I was eleven, I began to question life. I reflected many times that his passing opened my whole being to the inquiry, "What is life?" Fifty-six years later, I continue the journey when blessed individuals invite me into the intimacy of their hearts during challenging times of changes. I know what it's like to freeze in midair, to hear the shocking news of a loved one's death. The physical loss of a loved one can be a spiritual initiation. Rare physical, mental, and emotional pain cause transmutation and transformation and offer the gift of compassion.

Dr. Thomas Hora defines compassion as "understanding the lack of understanding."[3] There are no words, only standing by people's side as they step through the fiery hoop of sudden change. Pema Chodron wrote, "Compassion is not a relationship between the healer and the wounded. It's a relationship between equals. Only when we know our own darkness do we then know our light."[4] Humbleness comes from the spaciousness of knowing we each are called and cradled in that which knows.

Embracing our darkness and knowing it's a part of the bigger picture of who we are as human beings give us humility. I refer to being humble by

[3]   T. Hora, *Compassion Booklet* (Orange, California: PAGL Press, 1985), 1.
[4]   P. Chodron, *The Places That Scare You: A Guide to Fearlessness in Difficult Times* (Boston: Shambhola Publications, 2001).

saying, "I only walk on water when it rains." Humility is a reflection of an inner knowingness. This inner knowledge is known as the heart brain. This inner knowledge of heart intelligence is the synthesis of the energies that are referred to as positive and negative currents of energetic light. It is light that shines through worldly challenges. You're aware of an unspoken cosmic connection to something greater.

I often find myself dancing in the crack between the worlds. The crack between the worlds is the experience of knowing and unknowing, it is also the space that is always present and cannot be defined by the rational mind.

This is my journey to becoming Wakaygli Wasi Wingyag, "Woman Who Dances with Lightning."

Life's Reflections

1. What are ways I have question life itself?

2. How has humility softened heart?

3. What roads am I exploring?

Prayer

In this moment, I quiet myself and listen to an inner voice proclaiming that all of life is connected. Life is eternally one. Everything in which I am is awakened to my holy knowingness. There is a glow of knowing that humbles me, and in my humbleness, all my needs are abundantly met. For this I am grateful and celebrate my divinity. I allow this inner voice to be my outer voice expressing gratitude for life.

"It is raining from the heavens and the earth is open and drinking the sweet nectar of the sky. Remember—feel your connection with the earth and sky. Be humble and be not afraid to walk upon the water. You will not sink into the mud but you will become one with the earth. See your cosmic reflection within the mirror of mind and breathe from your fiery heart of living union. We are a part of it all, we are all related."

PL

Part One

THE PATH OF THE FEATHER

A heart without dreams is like a bird without feathers.
—Suzy Kassen, *Rise up and Salute the Sun*[5]

---

5   S. Kassen, *Rise up and Salute the Sun* (Boston: Awakened Press, 2010).

Chapter 1

THE PATH OF THE FEATHER

In 1994, I had the opportunity to invite High Star, a well-respected spiritual leader of the Rosebud, Lakota Indian Nation, to speak and do a blessing for our spiritual community. People dressed like wannabe Indians gathered outside to participate in the ground blessing before High Star's talk. One man dressed in a leather jacket with beads and held a wooden staff. I saw others point and say, "I bet that's him!"

Five minutes before the blessing began, a lovely lady skidded a car with High Star inside into the parking lot. High Star, wearing jeans, a ribbon shirt, and Nike tennis shoes, stepped from the car. His long hair distinguished him as a joy-filled Native American leader; this man was full of charisma and presence. He taught Taoism around the world because he had discovered the ancient wisdom gave him patterns of nature. These were the same patterns in nature that his grandfathers had taught him. They were the magical messages of the ancient people.

After his presentation, I asked if I could study Taoism with him. He paused and then asked me to go away for the summer and pray about this. If it was right for me to study with him, I'd receive a sign. I said I'd be glad to pray about it. I took him back to the airport and thanked him.

During my drive back home, I found my rational mind on tilt while trying to figure out what the sign might be—or what he even meant by a sign. Every day I took it into my spiritual practice, praying for my highest path to be revealed to me.

That summer, I defied my husband's wishes and purchased a beautiful aspen grove on some mountain property. I felt I had purchased a piece of heaven. The land became my sanctuary, and during the summer, I traveled there every week on my day off. I called this sacred place Tall Trees. There was the fragrance of aspen bark, the sweetness of wild flowers. The aspens stood as white candles erected to the heavens.

I usually went late at night after teaching a class, and I drove by myself in my old, yellow Toyota pickup. I would carefully walk up the road and enter my tepee, which I had placed on the land; it was my castle in the woods. I remember how magical the tepee was during a full moon, and the tall aspens quaking in the night became a kaleidoscope, reflecting the flow of the full moon onto the tepee. The mountain meadows, aspens, and snow-topped mountains were my salvation, my place of retreat.

There was no cabin at Tall Trees, just an old porch someone had attempted to build. While I was removing a pile of fallen aspen leaves from the half-built porch, I uncovered a perfect, beautiful raven feather. I was in awe at the discovery. My rational mind said, *How in the world could this raven feather be tucked away so perfectly under moldy leaves?* I felt a shiver down my spine, and I could hear in my mind, "If you receive a sign, contact me."

Wow! Could this be the sign that I was supposed to study with High Star?

I held up the feather and saw the light touching the majestic alignment of each fiber on the feather. The feather was inviting me to trust the flight that my soul was about to experience. I didn't realize there would be a day in the future when I'd be called to dance with eagle feathers attached to my arms, giving thanks to creation for its magic!

Tom Cowan wrote,

> Some people know from their earliest days that they are called to lead a more intense spiritual life than their peers. This inner knowing may come from dreams or from an abiding sense that helping spirits are present and active in one's life, or from a strong desire to serve the community as a healer or wise one.[6]

---

[6]   T. Cowan, *A Pocket Guide to Shamanism* (Trevose, PA: Crossing Press, 1997).

I carefully placed the raven feather on the dashboard of my faithful, yellow Toyota pickup and traveled back to the city. My mind was still filled with awe. I knew I could humbly behold the path of the feather within my heart. I placed the feather carefully on my personal altar when I got home and continued to contemplate the enormity of the invitation to study with High Star.

The next morning, I placed a phone call to High Star to arrange a date to meet with him.

There wasn't a lot of logic to explain my five-hour drive to New Mexico. I crested a mountain pass and drove down into the rust-colored rolling hills, trusting every turn was a letting go and a sense of adventure. I soon understood that the rational mind played tricks on us, and I had to trust a deeper mind.

High Star's home was warm and inviting, just like his smile and corny sense of humor. Friends familiar with Native American traditions told me to offer tobacco to High Star as I approached him. I offered him my package of Prince Albert tobacco. He sat and loaded his prayer pipe with tobacco. The smoke spiraled upward as he softly sang and prayed. The smoke from his pipe was the visible breath of the Creator. I found this to be sacred and amazing. I sat beside him and thought, *What if he doesn't accept me as a student?* My ego was intimidated by the stillness that seemed to last forever. This wasn't like the world I was accustomed to where I'd sign on the dotted line in five minutes or less and receive a ticket.

Piercing the silence, he said, "I want you to fast for a week, and I'll take you as one of my students of Taoism." He looked into my eyes and continued. "I'm inviting you to attend this summer's Sun Dance as a supporter."

He gave to me the name of a lady who would teach me what I needed to know about how a woman entered the Sun Dance experience. I thanked him, popped back into my old truck, and headed home. In future moments of contemplation, I had no idea of the enormity of the invitation. High Star's invitation to be a prayer supporter at Sun Dance came as a surprise. How did he know I held a sincere interest in the ancient ways of the Native Americans?

5

When I arrived home, I went into the bedroom, laid my head on my pillow, and gave thanks for the magic appearance of the raven feather and the special invitation I had received. I was glowing with gratefulness, knowing the presence of the holy, wise, and great teacher. I couldn't possibly explain to my family how I was feeling. I sensed they would see it as one of my crazy fantasies. I was known for sitting out on a limb of a tree, staring at the stars, and trying to connect the stars together like a big connect-the-dot puzzle. Now something bigger was happening to me.

The following years with High Star and the Lakota people would be the greatest test of faith and trust for me, but they built a platform of commitment that I'd never known before in my life.

Life's Reflections

1. Do I resist connecting the dots because I doubt? Because I fear myself?

2. Do I resist connecting the dots because it asks me to detach from my selfish ways of perception?

3. Do I resist connecting the dots because it's simple, and I learned to work hard and have things be heavy and burdensome?

Prayer

Holy, divine presence that is breathing me, I accept that magic moments are the spontaneous alignment and synthesis of intentions. Life is one big design. Everywhere I look, I see the perfection of God. I let this inner knowing be my compass this day and every day. Today I'm guided and directed, and I accept the good of life that is all around me.

Chapter 2

THE SOFT DOWN OF YOUR BELLY

He who looks outside, dreams; who looks inside, awakes.
—Carl Jung

 "We have walked together in the shadow of a rainbow and danced the beams of light within our dreams."

Life seems to be one big puzzle, and it is our job to put the pieces together to connect the symbols. It's up to us to see our bigger purposes and the themes of our lives.

I had always dreamed in color, and sometimes my dreams would be like a Metro-Goldwyn-Mayer production. But I had never experienced a lucid dream. Lucid dreaming is where you cross the crack between the worlds. Quantum science may refer to it as being in a parallel universe; it illumines beyond time and space.

The bear has always been a symbol of healing strength for me. Shortly after meeting with High Star, the bear came to me to offer greater spiritual awareness. This was when I met my most respectful friend, the bear. Did I know I'd be asked to bare my soul through the open portals of bear wisdom?

That evening, I drifted from a conscious, awakened state to a vivid space within the dream world with the bear. I closed my eyes, and there was bear. I opened my eyes, and there was bear. I journeyed within that experience and recorded the chapter titles that the bear gave me that night.

Within my dream time and awake time, I smelled the bear and felt its coarse, black fur. I went beyond the coarseness of his hair to find myself leaning into the softness of its belly; it was like being on a soft dream pillow. Then our noses touched, and I could hear its jaws clicking as we stared into each other's eyes. The raw, earthy smell was intoxicating and almost hallucinatory. It opened my nostrils, cleared my sinuses, and opened me to a place of great visions.

I consulted with High Star regarding this powerful dream. High Star said, "What will you do if a physical bear appears to you? You'll become one with it." His question was something I had thought about a hundred times on the mountain. High Star also said, "The physical bear can turn furious if it's ill or placed in a defensive situation. Be careful on your journeys to the mountaintop."

> Your visions will become clear only when you can look into your
> own heart. Who looks outside, dreams; who looks inside, awakes.
> Let my dreams be bigger than my fears. And my actions
> louder than my words.[7] —Chi Miiguich

Mayto Akapa (Big Bear) was my teacher in the dream time and on the mountain top. All I had to do was to still myself and address the bear as Dear, Most Respectful Friend, and the bear would speak to me.

Trusting in this greater dimension of mystery and magic has assisted me in understanding how life's fibers are woven together. In her book *Eat, Pray, Love*, Elizabeth Gilbert wrote, "To find the balance you want, this is what you must become. You must keep your feet grounded so firmly on the earth that it's like you have four legs instead of two. That way, you stay in the world. But you must stop looking at the world through your head. You must look through your heart, instead. That way, you will know God."[8]

The bear has taught me to listen with my feet, salute my instinctual abilities, trust my intuitive nature, and look through my heart.

---

[7] C. Miiguich, *Memories, Dreams, Reflection* (New York: Vintage Books, 1989).

[8] E. Gilbert, *Eat, Pray, Love* (New York: Viking, 2006).

Life's Reflections

1. What is dreaming me?

2. What does dreaming with the moon mean to me?

Prayer

This day, I accept my instinctual and intuitive nature. I open in heart to listen to harmonious celestial choirs, singing and dancing creation. I'm intoxicated with the love of the Creator. I give thanks for what has dreamt me.

I reflect upon my respect for all of life, and I give thanks for tall trees, mountains, and the sea of Love-Intelligence.

"You must go through the forest of your mind, trust the mystery of the night and bask in the warmth of the sun of day. In your world, the word *scary* means dangerous. I observe you are having an outrageous and wild fun time too! Now, what does scary, dangerous, outrageous, courageous, and fun have to do with the wilderness? The wilderness is constantly asking you to go the distance, and it gives to you the realization of your inner space in order to be present in the outer space of your reality. Your reality is no longer separated from the existing environment; your breath is the wind, and your feet connect you to a cosmic field that is magnetic in nature. You will walk on dry leaves until they turn to rose petals. Never forget that you lead with your heart as I do. Your senses of smell and sight in the night are your radiating rays of inner sight."

Chapter 3

TALL TREES

Being present at Tall Trees in the fall was a display of a pallet of nature's burnt umber, gold, yellow, and oranges. I could feel the unfolding of the warm colors around me. Tall Trees was my secret garden, and I continued to find many feathers, especially hawk feathers.

The magic continued, especially on the day I took my meditation teacher and his wife for a picnic to Tall Trees. We entered my small tepee dwelling. All of a sudden, a huge shadow covered the tepee. I looked up and saw, without equivocation, a big white bird not of this physical world. After the fact, High Star assured me that my friends and I had experienced a visit from the thunder beings.

What was a thunder being? I had heard about them in mythic tales and read about them in Indian lore. Would my path reveal the meaning of a thunder being to me? A teacher in graduate school said, "Patty, sometimes it is okay to leave something a mystery." I choose to be with it as a mystery. Once again, I danced between the cracks between the worlds.

The magic continued. I always closed the tepee's smoke flaps when I left for the city, so that rain or snow wouldn't enter the tepee. One weekend, I arrived at the little tepee. With the morning sunshine warming my back, I opened the flaps, tied them off, and entered the tepee. In the center of the fire pit, directly under the opening of the apex (which had been closed), was a beautiful hawk feather. How did it enter the structure—or did it simply manifest?

The bear was my teacher in dream time, and it was teaching me to trust the magical manifestation of feathers, stones, and the deep voice that continued to speak to me.

Life's Reflections

1. How do I define mystery?

2. How can I mine the gold of mystery?

Prayer

Today, I stand tall and reach for the heavens. I'm rooted in divine love, and I'm as flexible as a willow in the wind. I'm the living presence of beauty strengthened, and the majesty of divine magic is the radiance and the color of my being. I'm rooted in gratitude, glory, and grace.

Chapter 4

WHAT IS THE WILDERNESS?

 "What is wilderness? All of life is the wilderness. The wilderness is vast and truly unknown by the frailties of man. Only the stout-hearted enter to feel the gentle strength of what has been unknown to humanity. It is my home. The high tundra, the snow fields of diamond glee. The smell of earth is like the smell of a living grandmother's bosom as she rocks you to sleep. There is an eternal beat or drone that is like the bass drum. The orchestration of sound, the songs of birds, and the roar of the drone of the earth makes up the scene. It is the synthesis of vibration and the degrees of color as the hues light my day. I sleep under the galactic sky, and I never ask why."

I now had two tepees on the Tall Trees property. It was a safe residential mountain property and was the perfect place for me to stretch my wings of independence. I was respectful with the placement of my tepees on my four acres of property, but my neighbor must have complained about the horse tail that acted as a wind shock flying from the tallest pole of the large tepee. I received a form letter from the homeowner association that stated the tepees were not a sound architectural structure. I found this letter amusing because tepees withstand tremendous storms and have been the homes of Native Americans for hundreds of years.

I quieted my mind from the chatter of sensing that Tall Trees did not feel safe. The quaking aspens were like a hundred little voices saying I needed to be free. I chose to vision and pray, and stayed open to greater possibilities. I set my intention and affirmed there would be a place for me on the mountain where I would be able to be free, have my tepees, and experience spiritual ceremonies.

Within a couple of weeks, I saw a for sale sign on the dirt road leading into Tall Trees. It read, "Ten acres, national forest and mineral rights." Within a month I sold Tall Trees for cash and purchased the ten acres on the national forest land. How fun it was to own a mining claim with a mining deed that had been inscribed with a quill pen in 1887!

Margaret Tobin Brown, the unsinkable Molly Brown, wanted her own silver mine. The Molly in me smiled to think I would have my own silver mine. *The Unsinkable Molly Brown* was a great inspiration for me as I grew up. Unsinkable Molly Brown would say, "I ain't down yet." How many times did I become the Unsinkable Molly Brown? My Molly attitude kept me out of summer school when I was a child so that I could play on the mountain during the summers with my brother and cousins. I liked Molly's determination to make it in life; this gave to me true grit to step forward on my path as a child during difficult times. Now, the Molly who lived inside of me would have her very own mine and mountain to care for.

In his book *Awakening*, Mark Nepo wrote, "Our journey of life is not about travel but being about the swim through experience that expands our understanding of life. The swim also extracts our gifts from us."[9]

The new property was a gift to me.

Friends came to help me move thirty-four tepee poles, each seventeen feet long, from Tall Trees up a twisty jeep road to their new location on the mountain. I went from a fairly safe environment to the top of the mountain in the midst of national forest land. I was isolated and free, and I soon discovered my neighbors were bears. The strong winds, howling coyotes, and a bunch of fears raised my senses to a new norm for transformation. I was in for many lessons trusting my pathway. My new neighbors, the bears, left calling cards of bear scat and claw marks on the mighty pine trees.

The dirt road to my mountain property crossed a mountain stream. Before crossing the stream with Yellow Bird, my old rusted yellow Toyota pickup, I stopped no matter what the weather was like, got out, and offered tobacco to the earth. I saluted the six directions as my Native American

---

[9]   M. Nepo, *The Book of Awakening* (Newburyport, MA: Conair Press, 2011).

friends had taught me. My prayer was, "May this mountain always be sacred to all who enter its majesty." I added to my prayers the blessing of the Great Bear Spirit. It was important that I always approached the mountain with respect.

I think the old Toyota enjoyed cooling its tires as we slowly walked our way through the stream bed. Something about stopping at the stream to pray was magical. The prayers were received and appreciated by the Great Bear Spirit. The truck and I would slowly climb the weathered, rutted, and rocky narrow path up the hill.

This wasn't a mountain subdivision—this was the wilderness. I rationally knew that the word *wild* didn't mean out of control or to haphazardly destroy. In life, we are asked to trust what is wild and organic. The wilderness of humankind's very own soul is the last undiscovered wilderness. It calls us to define our personal wilderness through the facility of our awakened conscious states. We need to cross the bridge of imagination to discover our inner integrity. The word *wild* means to touch the true integrity of our beings.

Integrity is a state of being unimpaired and being organically aligned with the truth of who we are as spiritual beings. Living a life of integrity is to live our natural God-given life. Integrity is posed within each of us to walk the talk and to learn to trust in the invisible that brings forth the visible. Integrity demands honesty in thought, action, and word. In order to live within our natural lives, we are asked to show up, tell the truth, and align with an inner composer.

Every day spent on the new mountain site was a day of discovery, whether it was the beautiful sunrise, the sculptured trees that had been chiseled by chilling winds of winter, or laying on my back and watching the clouds move. At night, the stars at this high altitude were a galactic ocean of white light.

The first summer on top of the mountain, I carefully placed my tepee close to the forest service's rugged Jeep road. It felt safe being close to the road even though the road was remote and in the midst of the Pike

National Forest of Colorado. The following summer, I moved my tepee deeper into the forest and placed it next to a serene mountain spring. It was a spring that fed into the lower stream that I crossed on my drive to the top of the mountain. Moving the tepee farther into the forest was a test. I had always been a curious child, but as an adult, it had been important to discern my choices and play it safe. Now, I felt as though I was living on the edge of uncertainty, and I needed to create a stronger edge within myself in order to enter into a new frontier.

My first night next to the stream in my smaller tepee was a test of bravery. My mind raced like an Olympic track star, and I worked to calm my mind. I wrote in my journal and affirmed I was not alone. My spoken thought immediately manifested: I was not alone. A group of coyotes surrounded the tepee and began to howl. *Oh, God!* I thought. Without further thought, I began to howl back. I never thought I'd be in a choir with coyotes. Everything became super silent, and I didn't hear them again that evening. I'm sure the coyotes are still talking about the night a strange, two-legged coyote outrageously howled at them.

I wish I could report that the experience of howling with the coyotes brought me to a mystical state of singing the universal song of living oneness. After contemplating the experience, I was pole-vaulted out of a place of fear. It opened me to a deeper trust and communion with my nature. I imagine howling in the midst of city traffic would not produce the unity that I experienced that night. This would be one of many trust walks across the bridge of fear to embrace my inner wisdom.

Once, when I wasn't physically present on the mountain, a bear clawed the tall tepee lodge pole, which was secured to a larger pine tree waiting for my second tepee to be erected. The bear also clawed the canvas of the one standing tepee. I cut a bear claw patch from a scrap of canvas and sewed it to the canvas with sinew. I hoped it would be my communication to the bear that I was its new neighbor. To this day, the bear patch remains on the tepee canvas.

Life asks us to jump from places of edgelessness and to move into the forests of our minds. Mythology refers to going back to our places of origin. Sometimes we are afraid to trust that the forests of our minds know how to provide and nurture us. It asks us to surrender and become a part of the forest, to become a part of what is organic and real.

This is the lesson of harmony: become one with the thousands of forests and the verses they sing. My Most Respectful Friend the Bear shared with me, in my moments of stillness, that I should listen to life with my feet and with my heart open to the awe and wonder. I was able to explore the boundaries of my nature.

My wilderness experience demanded that I be open and expand my window of instinctual seeing. I needed to trust my intuitive nature. The bear said, "Listen to your feet and have one antenna toward the sky." I chose to stay in a prayerful place of respect, to listen, and to be open to seeing my reflection within the clear mountain spring that gifted the bear and me with water.

All of life is perceived with mirrors. Windows, doors, and reflective ponds stand before us as reflecting pools of spiritual seeing. There are many mirrors in life. Several of them are known as smoky mirrors because they are fogged with judgments, resistance and anger, and the beliefs of whoever raised us. The mirrors also reflect what's lost, given away, or taken from us. Other mirrors are self-preservation and darkness and include the mirror of the moment.

Full integration and greater understanding of the spiritual kingdoms comes from spiritual seeing. For example, as humans we tend to view life through a lens of thinking, calculation, and an operational approach. There is nothing wrong with being a keen thinker, but we have to be willing to open the window shade of feeling. When we open the window of feeling, we don't lose ourselves; instead, we perceive a texture and color that we wouldn't have thought about or sensed, felt, or known with just our thinking awareness.

Can we be instinctual without feeling? Our natural instinct as human beings is to awaken through the windows of reasoning and feeling, of image and instinct. Trusting our keen gift allows it to lift us beyond the ego mental construct urges to awe; there is a softening of personal awareness of spiritual presence. The spiritual awe threads the needle and weaves in and through the golden tapestry of wisdom.

The wisdom of image sees beyond the objects or obstacles on our path. It calls for focusing on wisdom. Wisdom is having discernment of what is true and right. It knows there's a pattern of continuous good no matter the present circumstances.

The instinctual way of seeing opens us to our bodies' wisdom. My spirit friend, the bear, instructs us to be aware of our environment by listening with our feet. The windows of reasoning, feeling, image, and instinct are available to us. The cosmic kaleidoscope reflecting the prisms of cosmic truth are found through our individual viewfinders, and we begin to take in the living sense of a cosmic reality.

We have many dimensions of seeing, knowing, and being. Our life experiences assist us in polishing the window from the inside out, so we can see clearly the spiritual truth of who we really are. "Life is a mirror and will reflect back to the thinker what he thinks into it."[10] All of life is a mirror and reveals who we really are as cosmic points of light and spiritual seeing. Eligio Stephen Gallegos, a brilliant teacher and therapist and the author of *Animals of the Four Windows,* wrote,

> The four modes of knowing are: thinking, sensing, feeling, and imagery. Knowing through thinking is the window in which we, as humans, spend the greatest amount of time and energy. It is the dimension of ourselves with which we most strongly identify. Within it, we pin down that which becomes a substitute for the experience of Being. We have been trained to focus so intensely on thinking that we tend to lose sight of those other modes of knowing, the ones that do not differentiate us so keenly from one another and from our animal brethren.[11]

---

[10] E. Holmes, *Science of Mind* (New York: G. P. Putnam's Sons, 1966).
[11] E. S. Gallegos, *Animals of the Four Windows* (New Mexico: Moon Bear Press, 1991).

We have the availability to reason through the window of thinking and to open to the windows of imagination, feeling, and imagery. Many of us focus on the window of thinking and touch feeling, imagination, and imagery much less. It is important to touch into thinking, feeling, imagination, and imagery because they are inner senses and are lenses of creative life.

The new mountain property was living up to its name, Medicine Mountain. There was an unexplainable sense of healing energies. Have you ever felt that you were being watched, but there was nothing there physically that you could see? There were days like that on the mountain, but I never felt afraid. I began to understand why the symbol of the bear fetish always had an arrow pointing to the center of the bear. This was what I began to call high heart. The bear is a great healer and a being of introspection. I knew that the bear spirit was coming to me from the sacred place of high heart. Dr. Ernest Holmes taught, "Healing is the perception of wholeness."[12] The bears' presence gave to me a greater spiritual perspective of myself and others. I found my physical body to be strong, and even a tiny cut on my hand healed immediately.

Friends instructed me to read everything I could about bears. I was aware of their habits and mannerisms. As High Star said, I was physically careful. I carefully cooked and stored food. I didn't want to tempt the bear so that his or her natural patterns were changed. I taught friends who visited to be respectful and aware. I even carried a cow bell as I walked through the woods by myself.

You've probably heard this story of the bear bell. The national park rangers were advising hikers in Glacier National Park and other Rocky Mountain parks to be alert for bears and take extra precautions to avoid an encounter. They advised park visitors to wear bells on their clothes so they made noise when hiking. The bell noise allowed bears to hear them coming from a distance so that they would not be startled by a hiker accidentally sneaking up on them; this might cause a bear to charge. Visitors should also carry a pepper spray can just in case a bear was

---

[12]   E. Holmes, *Science of Mind* (New York: G. P. Putnam's Sons, 1966).

encountered. Spraying the pepper into the air would irritate the bear's sensitive noise, and it would run away. It was also a good idea to keep an eye out for fresh bear scat so one have an idea if bears were in the area.

People should be able to recognize the difference between black bear and grizzly bear scat. As the park ranger would tell people with a grin, black bear droppings are smaller and often contain berries, leaves, and possibly bits of fur. Grizzly bear droppings tend to contain small bells and smell of pepper.

What is life if you don't have humor to add balance to your life? We want to have equality with humor, and we do not want to kill joy. While in sacred ceremony with High Star, I learned to flex and not be so serious. Humor has a way of bringing balance to an experience.

Life's Reflections

1. What are ways to soften fear and to claim my inner power?

2. How do I jump from fear to faith?

Prayer

In this moment, I enter into the divine forest of divine mind. I quiet myself in honor of the life that lives above me, below me, and in and through me. With great humility, I accept my union with the great Creator. I'm tuned to hear, sense, feel, and see the knowing of the heightened frequencies of my divine atonement. I am grateful for tuning into the action of spirit, which is love. All is well within the kingdom of the divine.

On Medicine Mountain

by Barry Ebert and Patty Lucas Luckenbach

On medicine mountain,
The wind's blowing high.
Dancing survivors raise their prayers to the sky.
I hear yellow thunder way up high,
Listen to the hawk cry.

There is a place known as Medicine Mountain.
Up high where the wind blows strong,
It touches everything and chisels with cold ice the trees of long ago.
These medicine trees raise their foreheads to the sky;
They've stood tall in the thunderbolts of time,
Barely rooted to the earth,
A sacred resting place for birds to take birth and flight.
Every rock and flower flavors the hillside with the gentle scent of dawn
As grandmother earth gives birth with her water.

We're walking in the footsteps of wizards and fools,
Working with the same tools.

On Medicine Mountain, the wind's blowing high.
Dancing survivors raise their prayers to the sky.
I hear yellow thunder way up high,
Listen to the hawk cry.

The bears are a constant presence here;
At even tide, you can hear them pray as they run and play.
They bring their healing to the night,
Leaving their marks and their love in the bark of the trees.
The stars shine and the spirit sings;
With power and grace, the great elk pace
And share their mystery with the earth.
When you travel inside, you can feel the connection with all of life;
The wellspring of peace is here.

Part Two

THE PATH OF HEART

May the words of my mouth be the words of my
heart, acceptable in the sight of the Infinite.

Chapter 5

Trust the Journey

 "Naked and unafraid, my soul has lain upon a sunny branch of a mighty tree to surrender and to melt into the sun. I felt the sun behind the sun, offering a bridge of greater understanding—a reflection of something bigger than I had known."

The same summer I purchased land and mining claim in the national forest, I went on a life-enhancing journey to the reservation, to witness the Lakota Sun Dance. I was instructed that being a supporter meant praying for those who were Sun Dancing in the hot sun. I also learned that it was a lot of work keeping the camp for the dancers.

Once again, I was going this one alone. My then-husband didn't want to hear anything about my ventures into sacred rituals. I needed to trust the journey and walk it alone. I remember packing my truck with a borrowed one-man tent, my sleeping bag, and enough food for ten days. I packed my Bunsen burner to cook on, and I appreciated my many years as a Girl Scout. I never thought I was about to enter into an experience of survival and surrender that would draw my love for nature from the depth of my soul.

The experience of the Sun Dance took my framed memory of scouting and broke it into a thousand pieces. I was about to dance between the cracks of moon and sun; I had before me the opportunity to respect an ancient way and learn what surrender really meant.

High Star knew of a couple who was driving to South Dakota to attend the Sun Dance, and so he arranged for me to meet them and follow them to the reservation. I soon learned that the lady I was following up to Sun Dance was an adventurous woman. She was a very outspoken medicine woman and a powerful sun dancer. Her husband was big and strong, and a good friend of High Star's.

She drew me out of my shell by asking, "Do you like blueberry pie?" I replied that I loved it and that it had been my grandpa's favorite. She said, "Then eat it!" There was no pie present but I got what she meant: dive into my soul and eat away everything that was not soulful. I tapped into my need to trust my inner integrity, and it didn't matter whether the others liked blueberry pie. It was my pie and my path of soul.

I felt as though I was traveling a familiar path. I was coming home to a life and a people who had lived from the heart of Grandmother Earth for thousands of years and slept at night on the golden fields, as my friend the bear did. The day we drove up was alive with a deep prairie peace that danced through the grasses and the rolling Sandhills of Nebraska, stimulating my imagination to remember a time long ago when the Indian people were servants to this land and the land served them. On the fence posts were the raptors who had not forgotten the wisdom of the sky and earth. This land was ancient with history and stories of honor and glory. It would be the space where I could dive into my soul and metaphorically eat the blueberry pie. I also felt the bear's silly presence: it was as excited as a child coming home. As I approached the painted water tank of the little mission town, tears flowed down my cheeks. That evening I placed my head on the ground and felt the heartbeat of the ancient ancestors. I was home!

I entered a reality where time was only a measurement of a field of unity. You'd not succeed as a watch salesperson on a reservation. White folks kid around and say, "Its Indian time." The Native American doesn't have a clock in his or her head. The clock is the sun and the cycles of the day. Theirs is a feminine sense of time that is spaciousness. The Wicahcala (white folks) expect things to run on time, and if they don't, something is wrong. I realized that I was stepping into a place with a different experience of time, so I placed my watch in the glove box of my truck. Wicahcala also expected there to be an online class, or at least a seminar. There weren't any.

The first day of hot sun on my tent completely melted my deodorant. Thank heavens the toothpaste survived! Makeup ran down my face. I soon understood wearing facial makeup was a joke; the great Creator asked me to not mask my beauty. I became aware that makeup was my mental mask of what I thought I should look like for others.

My first Lakota Sun Dance was an eye-opening experience. I knew historians, actors, and movie producers never could afford what it takes to capture the simple sincerity of the vista and the hearts of the people—not that it would be allowed by the indigenous people. The well-known actor Kevin Costner was taken to the Rosebud Lakota Reservation to film the Academy Award–winning movie *Dances with Wolves*. He was humbled, and over the years, he has held a place of reverence and dignity for the Native Americans. He too felt the sacred.

Life's Reflections

1. What do I trust?

2. What are ways do I express your authentic self?

Prayer

Today, I trust the journey. There is always guidance and an openness embracing each moment that brings us home to heart. From the heart, I salute the divine journey. I am grateful for each step of my path of heart.

Chapter 6

COMING FULL CIRCLE

 "I don't chase my tail like some animals, but I do curl into a circle and sleep deeply all winter. The sleep is a part of my cycle. Rest is spiritual; please pause on the path and sense your balance. I stand tall as I emerge when the sun is high in the spring sky."

I like the concept of the bear emerging from its hibernation and bringing back into the circle the remembrance of its deity. I felt like I was emerging from an inner den of unconscious sleep time. Everything was new, yet everything had a familiar feeling to me. Had I walked this walk before? I had come full circle, back to an ancient ceremony to witness the power of circle.

The people in my camp were accepting and kind, but I think they were laughing at my little Bunsen burner cook stove. I arrived self-contained, just like one would have purchased a "Patty Kit" off the shelf. When I arrived, I was told we all put our food together in the cook shack. We cooked for everyone in the camp.

In the Wicahcala world, we all have our possessions and stuff and do whatever we need to do to protect our stuff. We plan and are good at predicting outcomes. The Native American world puts things together, like a beautiful patchwork quilt to be shared. The women gather patches of aunties' old dresses, borrow thread, and put it all together into a quilt. If you have a potato or two, and someone has the pot, then you serve everyone, and no one is left wanting. So much for my tiny cans of tuna fish and dried beans. This continued to be a lesson in accepting and working with everyone in the circle. There was no "mine or yours." It was a community participating together. To this day, some of the people in that first cooking experience are my best friends.

The men and elders were served first, and the children always had a place in the camp. I was told no photos or recording, so that my heart would stay focused on what was at hand. There was so much preparing for the dance. Sage crowns, anklets, and wrist bracelets needed to be prepared for the dance, as well as readying the prayer pipes. Then there was the physical basking each day in the Inipi steam purification ceremonies before the dance began.

Every day for the four days leading into the dance, at noon we'd gather to hear the stories of the elders and leaders of the dance. I learned quickly there were no instruction sheets passed out, and neither were there books to read. We listened to the stories, and the guidance was presented. The wisdom poured forth from the spiritual dance leaders who had mediated and prayed daily for months, asking the spirit world to help them remember the ancient ceremony of their grandfathers.

The traditional ceremony of Sun Dancing had been considered wrong and pagan by religious ministers and priests. The government was determined to push their civilized ways on a people who knew everything about living together in a community that fostered peace. For one hundred years, between 1879 and 1978, the Native Americans didn't have religious freedom. Many were arrested for praying and dancing as their grandparents had.

Alex White Plume organized the Memorial Big Foot Ride commemorating the one hundredth anniversary of the Battle of Wounded Knee, and he wrote, "For over 100 years, we've suffered and been a defeated people. After the 1890 Allotment Act, our horses were taken away. Our people were placed on reservation. Our religion was forbidden, and our language was outlawed. Everything went underground."[13]

I remember the day before the dance began. An alarmed Native American man came into camp to announce that the FBI was at the gates of the Sun Dance to collect eagle feathers from the white people (Wicahcala) who had been gifted a feather by Indian elders. The Indian man went camp

---

[13]   V. Deloria, *Vision Quest* (New York: Crown Publisher, Inc., 2006), 30.

to camp, wanting to gather the feathers of the Wicahcala and hide them from the FBI. Chief Albert White Hat Sr., one of the spiritual leaders of the dance, gathered everyone and said, "If they take a white man for a feather I have gifted them, they will take all of us. I have the right to pray and sing with all my brothers." His courage came from the depth of a healed lion's heart. He echoed truth for all people as he spoke. The FBI did not enter that day. How easy it is to become intimidated and fearful; speaking truth frees us all.

I continue to have a great appreciation for the leaders who stood before me. Their grandfathers and great grandfathers are in the textbooks, and their names are on monuments. These men told of going to the graves of their ancestors, meditating and praying to remember the meaning of the ceremonies, and they listened for guidance and signs.

The first morning of the dance, the Indian men who had been in camp and the leaders (including High Star) were dressed in their traditional garments. I felt that I'd been transported back into an ancient time. A beautiful young girl with hair as black as a raven's wing carried Hollow Horn Bear's pipe and led all the dancers into the circle to drum, sing, and dance their prayers.

The great Hollow Horn Bear Chief had gone to Washington D.C. in 1933 with other Lakota tribe members to attend President Theodore Roosevelt's annunciation. While he was in Washington, he fell ill and died of pneumonia. His family in South Dakota waited months for the body to be returned to them. It was a tremendous insult to the family and Lakota people to discover that when his body was returned, his eagle bonnet, beaded leathers, and prayer pipe were not with his body. The biggest insult was that he was dressed as a Wicahcala.

Approximately seventy-two years passed, and one day there was a phone call to the Hollow Horn Bear family saying, "We want to meet with you." You can imagine that the family held close the barbs of hurt and disrespect. When the call came, the family refused. But one day, the grandma said, "Go and see the gentleman." With trepidation, the great grandson of Hollow Horn Bear journeyed to meet with the gentleman.

The Wicahcala wanted to gift back to the family Hollow Horn Bear's prayer pipe. The story was that the gentleman's father had bought the pipe from a museum back east, and the father had died. The gentle son chose to do the right thing and return it to the people. Returning the pipe to the people was the sign to pray, meditate, and listen to those who had gone before them and were living in the spirit world. They learned how to resurrect the power of the Sun Dance.

The subtle, unspoken lessons of forgiveness were present within the multicolored hues of the morning. Forgiveness means that the past will never change. Give your energy to the moment and stand tall in the sun. Speak your name, knowing the Creator knew your name long before you took birth on the planet. For the Native American, forgiveness is a daily practice of breathing deeply the breath of the Creator and finding peace.

At the end of my first day of supporting and praying, High Star asked me what I had seen. Tears immediately filled the inside of my body, and I replied, "I saw a crucifixion and resurrection and rebirth." I had witnessed the healing power of surrender, and a grace that trumped a hot summer sky and gave wholeness and health.

The great poet Rumi wrote, "Don't turn your head. Keep looking at the bandaged place. That's where the light enters you. And don't believe for a moment that you're healing yourself."[14]

Life Reflections

1. What are ways in which I can see others as a part of my soul?

2. Who do I need to forgive this day, so I can remember who I am?

---

[14]   C. Barks and M. Green, *The Illuminated Rumi* (New York: Penguin Random House, Inc., 1997).

Prayer

May all men and women be free to dance and to pray. May love and forgiveness be a daily ritual. I forgive all who have taken, stolen, and robbed themselves of dignity and self-respect. May I give to myself and others only love. Love is the universal language of all people. The memory of gratitude lives within all hearts.

Chapter 7

STITCHING PRAYER—
SEEKING VISION

A bed without a quilt is like the heaven without stars.
—Anonymous

The currents of visions were like the Aurora Borealis, illuminating my dreams and my waking hours. The voice in my dreaming was vivid and repeating, "Go to the hill."

At the conclusion of the eight-day ceremony, I approached High Star once again. He listened, and I knew he was going to say something profound. He asked, "Are you crazy?" It was a test for me. I asked whether this was just my ego, or whether I truly following my heart. I was being called to go to the hill, which meant a vision quest. He said, "Patty, these ways are not easy." He was certainly correct about that!

Did I need another sign from the winged ones? High Star said, "Pray on this." I continued to pray and followed my heart. I was told it takes one year to prepare, and I had to begin by setting my intentions for the quest. My intentions for the quest were to experience perfect union with God and a physical healing for my daughter, who was at the time experiencing a brain lesion.

I began preparations for the Hanbleceya, the vision quest. A dear friend, who was a master quilter, took me shopping for my favorite colors for the quilt. She coached me how to make a star quit. Ages ago, Indian grandmothers painted with the hues of vegetables and flowers, creating the eight-pointed star on the hides that graced their homes. There wasn't any other culture I knew of that created such beautiful quilts.

Over the years, the traditional eight pointed star designing predominates, but broken stars, double stars and sunbursts are also favorites. To the Lakota, the star represents knowledge. The Mourning Star symbolizes new beginnings or a new dawn. Stars mark the beginning and the end of the day and indicate the four directions. In many of the quilts, the tiny diamond shapes have been carefully arranged into the symbols important to the Sioux such as the buffalo, the eagle, tepees and pipes, feather headdress and medicine wheel.

The quilters of the Rosebud Reservation carefully choose the colors for each of their designs. Frequently the color combinations become individualistic expressions of these artists. In contrast, certain symbolic elements are always portrayed in the same color.

The color brown is often seen in the center of the design, or beneath the tepee, representing the earth and life in the plants of the earth. Yellow, red and orange are associated with the sun. When they are used at the center of a design, they may represent the colors of the fire at the center of every home. Blue is the color of the sky and is often the background of an eagle design.[15]

I selected colors that my spirit resonated with, but my stitching brought forth concern in regard to being placed stark naked on the hillside with only this quilt to cover my body. The underlying fear appeared, and I often said, "High Star was right: I'm crazy." Had I lost my mind? Fear entered

---

[15] *Rosebud Quilts and Quilters* (St. Francis, SD: St. Francis Mission).

my bones as I thought about standing on a hill in the cool night, naked and wrapped in this quilt while holding my prayer pipe.

I had been instructed that after the quest, I had to give away the quilt to another. I was not to covet it but to give thanks and gift it to another. I continued to commit and build on my inner will to meet this divine assignment. The native belief is that our physical bodies are the robes of our souls. Time gave me a greater belief that my naked body would be sustained.

I learned to appreciate the artistry of every stitch of the Native Grandmother. I had never made a quilt, and I learned that each stitch was a prayer. The Grandmothers leave a place within the quilt for Spirit to enter. My first quilt had several holes; indeed, I was assured of Spirit entering my quilt!

Was I making the quilt, or was it making me?

Life's Reflections

1. What are the colors I resonate with? Where do the colors live within my body?

2. What are ways I can celebrate the tapestry of my journey?

Prayer

Today, I rejoice in the knowing that we are each cut from the fabric of Love-Intelligence. My body is woven light and is a vase of radiance. There is a golden thread of light that is in and through all of life. My very breath is the golden light. Breathe through me, Great Spirit; breathe through me. Make the prayer as me.

Chapter 8

SEEKING VISIONS

**You go to the hill to seek perfect union with the Creator
and a vision may be the by-product.
Albert White Hat Sr.**

Albert White Hat Sr., Nathan Tube, Sicangu Lakota, was the grandson of Chief Hollow Horn Bear, the spiritual leader of the Sun Dance. His mother was born in Crow Indian territory, where her father had traveled to make peace with the traditional enemies of the Lakota. Albert White Hat Sr. was a good man. He worked to standardize the alphabet for the Lakota language, and he worked to serve his people's well-being and to remember the spiritual, ancient ways of ceremony. He was a consultant for a PBS documentary and was a Lakota translator for the movie *Dances with Wolves*. He left the planet with his written word inscribed in books so the Lakota people would not forget their language before the white man came West.

I remember how Albert and his family opened their home to other Native Americans traveling across the country. He and his wife would invite young adults from all races for the summer, and he taught them the Lakota's philosophy and culture. The medicine is their spirituality. It was Uncle Albert who said, "When I do the Sun Dance, I don't seek answers. When I fast up on the hill, I don't seek visions. I do those things with a decision already made. I go up on the hill. The visioning is for help with that decision. I Sun Dance asking for help with that decision. The vision that you seek on the hill is what's inside of you."[16]

Martin Luther wrote, "True humility does not know that it is humble. If it did, it would be proud from the contemplation of so fine a virtue."[17] The vision quest asks each of us to enter the forest of our minds. It asks us to be naked and unafraid, and to realize we are never alone, that we are part of it all. Vision questing humbles oneself before the Creator. The quester asks to be touched by the simplicity of the Creator's purpose for him or her. In days gone by, vision questing was a rite of passage for the young.

Life's Reflection

1. What is seeking to express through me?

2. What are ways I can go to the hill of my very own soul and pray?

Prayer

O Divine Breath, breathe through me what you have dreamt for me through me. Let me be one with the wind and rain, and let me dance with the moon. May I rest in the dawning of each day to awaken and ride the rays of the sun. I accept my divinity, and I'm open to the Creator making a vision through me.

---

[16]   V. Deloria, Jr., *Vision Quest* (New York: Crown Publisher, Inc., 2006), 30.

[17]   M. Luther, *Christmas Book* (Minneapolis: Augsburg), R. Bainton, ed.

Chapter 9

Two Strikes

 "Lightning and thunder, water, the winds that blow, and the mud of earth contain the four sacred elements of our world. A strong thunder and lightning storm is like a holy candle-lighting ceremony; it is a communion between heaven and earth. When you pray, the thunder beings smiles, and the air, water, fire, and earth speak through you. Never forget you are a harmonizer, a peacemaker. You bring balance to every occasion."

Fearlessness—the brown mud bubbling beneath the woven vines and tangled weeds. It rises with the rains and hides dormant as the sun shines once again. Strong and moist with the rain of my tears (fearlessness), above me is a cathedral of blue, reaching high, high into the sky. I dance in the sun and melt in the rain, only to rise again. Fearlessness, you grace me with the sacred elements of clay, water. I breathe you, and my heart is the kiln of fire that feeds and fires the sparks and makes my earthen pot. From the bubbling mud of my immortal, I humbly give thanks for myself as mud woman. I stand tall in the sun and dance in the rain. I am forever sacred.

On July 16, 1996, my life changed forever. I had fasted for four days with no food or water in order to experience my Hanbleceya, known as a vision quest.

The night before leaving for the reservation, I was the minister speaking at a Wednesday night service. I was in my second day of fasting. Before the service, I called High Star. We went through my story that I had to speak and think clearly, and I asked if I could I have some juice as a fluid.

Silence. "No. Just lean into your prayers, and you will be fine." Okay. The men's quartet was singing "Peace Is Like a River." Spirit does have a great sense of humor.

The next day, a good friend took mercy on me and drove me the five hundred miles to the reservation. It was a big deal for me to surrender and allow another person to take care of me.

I had pledged to stay on the hill with my quest for twenty-four hours. This meant a total of five days with no food or water. On the second day of fasting, I felt that every cell within my body was screaming, "Chocolate, chocolate!" The third day I got to a point where my insides were more at peace. The fasting had the effect of my head feeling disconnected from my body. I trusted my prayer invisibly provided clear water. The fasting was lifting me to a place of clearer spiritual seeing.

Upon arrival at the reservation, my friend made sure camp was established. It was my fourth day of fasting. I was instructed to rest and stay cool under the one and only tree that was in the camp. If one could lie still, one would begin to rest in the heavy South Dakota heat. Certainly no one was on a time table. The afternoon passed, and the sun was preparing to kiss the moon. The sky was clear, and the softness of twilight was surrounding us. The Holy Man, High Star, knew months in advance that bolts of lightning would dance on the hill the night I stood to pray.

Ever since the appearance of the coat of white feathers that had covered my little tepee, I have had respect and curiosity for the thunder beings. What I was learning from the stories of thunder beings was to be grounded, to have my feet on the ground, and to tell the truth. Thunder beings harmonize the heavens and bring change to the earth. They bring the sacred rain that washes the earth.

On the quest, there would be a time where I knew the experience of standing amid the rain, which was a sacred wash. On that night, it rained miracles and cleansed my soul.

My Lakota sister lived in a community on the reservation called Two Strikes. Her sweat lodge was where the people going to the hill went first. The afternoon was heavy with scorching heat, and here there were no trees for shade. High Star knew we all had fasted and asked us, the two light-skinned people, to crawl underneath my old pickup to get out of the sun. This was where I met Christian, who was from Switzerland, and he became an endearing friend. To this day, we kid each other and say we met when we were preparing to die.

We were dripping with sweat after being purified in the Inipi (rebirth) sweat lodge prayer ceremony, and we were taken silently from the Inipi ceremony. My clothes and shoes were taken, my star quilt was wrapped around me, and my prayer pipe was handed to me. I was instructed to only speak to the Great Creator, and no one was to speak to me.

My prayer pipe had been gifted to me and had a buffalo bone inlay of a lightning bolt on its stem. High Star's uncle had taught me how to walk with the pipe instead of carrying it on my sleeve. The prayer pipe was my confidant, my prayer partner; I was taught to hold it in strong prayer, to listen for life's good virtues.

The sun was setting, and my quilt felt like an old friend. The night was sweet with a grassy fragrance. I sat in the front seat of my truck, wrapped like a mummy in my quilt, and my friend started the engine. We began to rock back and forth on the bumpy dirt road. A smile came over my face, and I knew I was not alone. I heard the song of the meadowlark. I recalled my precious grandpa whistling the sweet call of the meadowlark as he and I walked through the prairie grasses together when I was a child. I sat back in the truck and rode the bumpy road to the top of the hill. There were several other friends who were also going to the hill that evening. The truck stopped, and I heard the sound of someone pounding choke cherry stakes into the ground. Supporters were preparing the Hocoka (sacred circle). My Swiss friend was placed on the hill a distance away from me.

I was placed in the Hocoka. I heard the stakes hammered into the ground, and the sound echoed in the night. I felt they were preparing for a crucifixion. I asked Grandmother Earth to graciously accept the stakes. I wrote a month later in my journal,

> Deeply within the cradle of my soul is a flame. Brightly it burns and turns and whirls and spins. This light expresses itself to the coolness of the night and warms and lights my path. Naked, I stand and reach for the stars. The light streams out into the moonlight, and the beloved takes my hand and gazes into my eyes and it enters my heart. Surely we are all one.

The red felt prayer ties, each with a tobacco offering that I had tied, were placed around the choke cherry stakes, creating the Hocoka. The prayer ties created the circumference of my circle. I was placed in the center while High Star stood in front of the established altar. He sang his final Hanbleceya song. He said, "You may die here tonight; nothing keeps you here but your will. Nothing will enter through the prayer ties to harm you, not from this dimension or any other dimension." No truer words were ever-spoken.

I felt the earth and the crushed grasses beneath my feet. I stood with only my quilt and prayer pipe, and I heard the sounds of the truck descending the hill. I stood and prayed, stating my intention for the healing of my daughter and to know perfect union with God. I was in a timeless space, but I did notice that as the sun set in the west, the wind began to whistle and blow. Immediately mosquitoes by the hundreds descended upon me. I was there to pray, not to kill insects. I began to make the sound of the third eye, "Eeee," which sounds just like a mosquitoes humming. After all, this was a vision quest. There was light flashing in the west. The wind opened its throat and sang from its belly, and the flashing lights rapidly approached.

There isn't any place on earth for a violent thunder and rainstorm quite like South Dakota. The wind whirled, and the rain let loose. My precious quilt, which I had made each stitch with a prayer, was drenched. The blessing was that the mosquitoes swam away. My thoughts were, *I might drown in the mud!* The flashing lightning grew closer, and I had to go down to the ground for safety. The earth and sky were clapping cymbals. Lightning was all around me. My supporters had left a tiny blanket that contained sage, which had been placed in the circle for me to stand on. I rolled the tiny blanket up that had been placed for me to stand upon, and I placed the tiny blanket to my chest for warmth.

Never taking my hands off the prayer pipe, I prayed, "Great Spirit, have compassion upon me." The lightning flashed around me. The last thought I remembered was, *I know many people are praying for me. Tunkasila, have compassion on me.*

Back at the camp, the storm was violent. My dear friend and prayer supporter reverted back to her Catholic upbringing and tied a cotton string rosary of sacred knots for me. The storm was so intense that no one from camp was able to travel up the road to check on me.

As I lay on the ground, the first bolt of light touched the ground, and the second bolt hit and pushed the earth up under my chest. To this day, I don't recall being cold or wet; I believe I was in a trance and was grounded in Great Spirit. I was later told that the storm was violent all night.

The dawn brought the light. The warmth of the sun with the dew of the earth warmed the Hocoka and I awakened quickly. I lived! I slowly brought myself to my elbows and sat up. As I faced the east, I saw a double rainbow, and to the west I saw approximately twelve elk below me. I also discovered that the lightning had touched the ground two feet in front of my prayer ties. Approximately three feet from my prayer ties in the east, the lightning had stuck the ground, again, outside my prayer ties. High Star was right: nothing entered the sacred Hocoka to harm me.

My Native American sister, Violet, came for me early in the day. She approached me and announced that I had received my vision. She placed my wet prayer ties in a tree nearby where her ancestors had hung theirs. Later she shared with me that where I was placed was a burial ground for little children. I sat in the humid grass amazed at the new day. I was wrapped in my muddy, wet quilt.

In silence I rode down the bumpy road to the Inipi sweat lodge located at Violet's home. I was placed into the sweat lodge along with a young

Lakota boy who had been on the hill for four days, fasting. The holy man, Uncle Percy, and other Lakotas gathered as the Grandfather Tonka's (hot rocks) were brought into the musty lodge. The prayers and heat felt good, and I never forgot when Uncle Percy gave me a cup of sacred water after five days without water. He said, "Sip, and now you know that water is sacred!" Uncle Percy gave me the name Wakaygli Wasi Wingyag: Woman Who Dances with Lightning.

The thunder beings brought balance and sacred rain the night of my vision quest. That night, the rain cleansed my soul, and because of their mischief, I'd earned my name.

When I emerged from the sweat lodge ceremony, my dear friend was there to hug me. With tears streaming down her cheeks, she said, "I thought I wouldn't ever see you again." She placed the rosary of tiny knotted string around my neck, which she had prayed with all evening for my safety. She indeed had connected the dots. We hugged like two old bears. Something incredible had happened. I had experienced perfect union with God, and my daughter was healed. I was received into the heart of the Lakota Nation.

My quilt was given to a good friend who had driven from the state of Washington to support my vision quest in prayer. I heard years after the fact that she wrapped her firstborn child in it. Daily I continue to walk the prayers of the prayer pipe.

We are all within the sacred Hocoka, and nothing can enter to harm us. We are the Hocoka, the great circle of life; our intentions are golden threads of interconnected acceptance. The light always comes before the thunders (Hanbleceya). Something transformed within me that evening. What changed? Was it moving beyond the illusion of fear and control? Was it the realization that I stand as the light of infinite presence? After the evening on the hill, the visions I received continued to unfold for me over a long period of time. The next summer I was called to Sun Dance. In later years, High Star shared with me that he knew I was good to dance because I was so dedicated to prayer; I wasn't attached to being a dancer.

The next summer I would Sun Dance for the first time. I definitely had experienced two strikes!

I continued to study intently with High Star for three more years. We worked together monthly over the phone. I continue to consult with him to this day. For me, he is an amazing teacher.

Years later, in my involvement with the Lakotas, I learned the meaning of using red felt to wrap my prayers ties. Not only was my Indian rosary of prayer ties using red felt, but a piece of tobacco twist rope was placed within the red felt. The thunder beings are attracted to red felt. Cherokee mythology holds that the number three is the Great Thunder and his sons, the two thunder beings who live in the land of the west above the sky vault. The priests prayed to the thunder, and the thunder beings visited the people to bring the rains and blessings from the south. It was also believed that the thunder beings who live close to the earth's surface, in the cliffs and mountains and under waterfalls, harm the people at times. Those thunder beings were always plotting mischief.

Life's Reflections

1.   How do I dance in the rain?

2.   Is there a way to experience perfect union with my God?

Prayer

Holy sacred divine mind and heart, I stand naked in the wind and connect my very being with the cosmic light of creation. My word is a ray of sun that brings forth growth and nurtures all existence. It is not about the storms of life, but knowing how to dance in the rain. I am grateful.

I Thirst

Put your fingers in water and touch them to your forehead.

Say to yourself out loud,

"Bless my understanding so that I may be here fully."

Touch the water to your eyes and say,

"Bless my vision so that I may see with clarity."

Touch your mouth with the water and say,

"Bless my mouth so that I may speak with truth."

Touch your heart and say,

"Bless my heart so I may feel."

Part Three

THE PATH OF INNER WISDOM

Chapter 10

DEEP ROOTS OF INSTINCT

After my first vision quest, I thought I'd bundle up my mother and take her to Medicine Mountain, my property in the national forest. My mother had financially assisted me when I'd purchased the property, and the kid inside wanted her to see the property. I also wanted to spend as much time with her as possible because her memory was melting away like chocolate on a hot summer day. I carefully maneuvered my little but mighty Toyota over the road. I had surrounded my elderly mom with pillows to protect her from the bumpy ride up Medicine Mountain.

She said to me, "Patty, I never know where you're taking me." Then we'd laugh and laugh. I knew it did her soul good to be outside in the fresh mountain air. I wanted to ask her as much as I could about my father, the love of her life, before her memory faded into the many sunsets of her life.

I was ten years old when my father died suddenly. My younger brother and I didn't speak about him around Mom because it made her cry, and we didn't need any more sadness in our little home. Eleven years after Dad's death, she remarried. We loved our stepdad and chose to have a living memory of our father in our hearts. We respected our stepfather and didn't ask a lot of questions about our father's death.

It's interesting how the primary instinctual impressions are never lost from our psyches. That night in 1996, when I was dancing with lightning, my supporter had placed a small blanket inside my circle (which I referred to as a medicine cloth) with sage and my prayer ties in it. I stood on it. When the storm developed, I took the small fabric, rolled it up, and placed it next to my chest, hoping it wouldn't be drenched in the rain. It stayed next to my chest all night. I always wondered why I did that.

While we bounced on the narrow dirt road, my mom spontaneously shared some details with me. "Your father, who suffered from head injuries from WWII, came home every day from the post office with migraine headaches. When you were a baby, you had a chronic upset stomach and cried the first year of your life. Your father would come home and sit in his favorite chair, and I would place your small body on his chest. You both would calm down and fall asleep."

I was finally able to connect the dots. I had rolled up the little blanket and held it secure in my calmness in the midst of dancing with lightning. I was able to connect my actions with how my father comforted me when I was an infant.

Instinctively, my primal connection and direction was established in the inner realms of being and the reservoirs of protectiveness that stimulate the alertness of the outer awareness. Thank you, Mom, for a good day on the mountain. The messages you shared with me remain forever with me, and I know they live within your soul also.

Life's Reflections

Close your eyes and still your mind. Ask the primal protector of your being:

1. Who has been my protector?

2. How do I keep safe and warm?

Prayer

In the beginning and forever, there is love. I honor my mother and father and all who carried me and loved me. In this moment, the Father of us all is breathing me and rocking me in loving arms. I'm protected, warm, and safe. The gentle and warm blanket of compassion heals me and sets me free.

Chapter 11

WE ARE THE LIGHT

 "We have walked together in the shadow of a rainbow and danced the beams of light."

Weeks after my experience of dancing with lightning, I drove to Medicine Mountain late one night. It was about an hour out of Denver, and I was swaying back and forth as I drove up the rocky dirt road. I heard two voices. One was my mother's voice saying, "I told you never to go by yourself at night." The other was spirit saying, "You're never alone."

It was after midnight when I arrived at ten thousand feet. I had a strong feeling that I should not enter the forest to sleep in my tepee, so I parked and climbed into the back of my covered truck. I reached for my battery lantern, and to my surprise, the lantern lit up before I placed my hands on it. I removed my hand, and the light dimmed. I approached it again, and it was as bright as ever. I was charged. I lay down in the back of the truck as the lantern glowed, and the moon shone overhead. I wasn't alone; there were orbs of light all around the truck. I awoke with the rays of the sun warming the truck. Once again, I had moved through the night with the light.

The day at Medicine Mountain was waiting for me, and so I greeted the sun, heated a cup of tea over my small camp stove, and secured my gear. I put my prayer pipe in my day pack and placed it on my back. I was eager to go down the hill and see my bleached white tepee with the Indian sign of "Oh Great Spirit" on its side.

I was reminded that my experience was not magical. It was the realization of what is true for each of us. Howard P. Bad Hand stated, "We are looking out through our own cosmic black hole through the multi-dimensional dynamics of the one life. All black holes have an inversion of light. It is as though I looked into the deep forest of mind a cosmic holographic universe."[18] I recognized that light shines above up and through each of us.

Dr. Ernest Holmes states, "Just as Moses saw the bush give light, so may you. This was not an illusion of his but a reality. At the center of everything there is fire, celestial fire, sought from heaven. Every bush would blaze if we unified with that central spark which is the cause of all involution and evolution, all advancement, everything we know, everything we shall ever attain."[19]

During the weeks that followed, due to the amount of electricity in my body, I had to replace my watch battery several times, and working with the computer was interesting. I learned to never doubt for one minute how powerful I was.

Life's Reflections.

1. What are ways I maintain my lightness?

2. The most powerful ways I shine my light are:

Prayer

I tune to the Infinite light of Spirit. I behold Spirit's light in and through all things. This holy light is life itself, adorning and radiating in and through my physical body and my body of affairs. The warmth of this light warms my soul. The light of God is above, below, and all around. Gratitude is the radiance of divine light.

---

[18]   Howard P. Bad Hand, Taoism Workshop, Denver, 2011.
[19]   E. Holmes, *Light* (Los Angeles: Science of Mind Publications, 1980), 15.

Chapter 12

ENTERING INTO THE DEN OF HEART

"What is man without the beast? If the entire beast were gone, men and women would die from loneliness of spirit for whatever happens to the beast also happens to men."[20] —Chief Seattle

 "You humans continue to think you are the epitome of civilized charitable behavior. When we talk about animals, you exclude yourself from the category, and you say someone is being like an animal with their disrupting, crude, chaotic behavior. You think you are the only species capable of compassion. I represent balance and transformation. I breathe in a circular motion, and my bones soften in hibernation like butter. I tuck myself in a cave or under a tree's root base to rest and pray."

When I returned to the mountain after pledging to dance the next summer, I noticed the handsome big tepee had been entered; the door was torn, and it was flapping in the wind. I immediately felt overwhelming fear. A bear, tall on its hind legs, had left its muddy claw marks above the door of the tepee. The bear could have taken down the tepee but didn't.

---

[20]   H. A. Smith, *Seattle Sunday Star*, October 1887.

A baby bear must have entered underneath the hem of the tepee, and Mother Bear had come to fetch it. I became especially careful because Momma bears are furious protectors of their young. My respectful friend, the Bear, gave me a powerful lesson and gift.

The bear had entered into my most cherished mountain dwelling place. Was this a sign telling me not to Sun Dance? Who was I to Sun dance? I knew I had a red heart, but I was a Wasicum Winyan, a white woman. I didn't want the Lakota community to think I was a wannabe trying to be an Indian or steal their ways. All of these thoughts came up as I thought about the meaning of the big bear entering my tepee. After I calmed myself, I received the gift from bear. He had entered my heart space.

In life, it's important to ask the right questions. In *Beyond the Dream,* Dr. Thomas Hora poses two intelligent questions we need to ask. The first question is, "What is the meaning of what seems to be?" The second question is, "What is really REAL?"[21]

The first question asks us to look at the mental thought and to not judge and blame, but allow the meaning in the present moment to be revealed. The second question asks us to switch to what is really REAL, referring to our spiritual connection and identity. I continued to learn that there's nothing too big for God.

Within the wildness of my human concerns, I discerned the situation and stepped back to observe and focus on what was real. I allowed love to lift me from any fear to what was REAL.

---

[21]   T. Hora, *Beyond the Dream* (New York: The Crossroad Publishing Company, 1996), 178.

Life's Reflections

1. What does "what is really REAL" mean to me?

2. What are the ways I nurture my heart and commitment daily?

Prayer

I am humbled in the sight of the love and the intelligence of creation. Creator, allow me to dance my prayer every day of my life. The stones upon my path have been washed by water, and trust has been written on them with invisible ink. I'm grateful to walk on water when it rains and to know my imprint signals. I trust!

Chapter 13

DANCING WITH THE SUN

 "How do I carry the power of the sacred? I carry the sacred bundle because I'm the sacred. It is not about how to do it; it is a realization that all of life is sacred. I stand on holy ground. I'm connected with all of life. The trees are my brothers and sisters. The manifested forms that come to you are from the sacred, invisible realities that surround you. You are not an isolated human. You hold with your field of awakening the holographic reflections of your species and the species known by the Universe. I reflect the light of the Pond. Your reflection of the pond is the cosmic universe."

People ask me what a Sun Dance is. I am respectful and choose to give them the truth that was shared with me by elders. The Sun Dance ceremony is one of the seven sacred ceremonies of the Lakota Sioux. The Sun Dancer sets intentions during the Winter Solstice preceding the full sun of summer when they will dance. It's a twelve-day ceremony beginning with four days of purification, utilizing the Inipi ceremony (sweat lodge) to purify one's being. The ceremony helps set one's mind to enter a heartfelt place to dance their prayers for four days. For the four days following the dance, the dancers remain in the sacred energy of the dance by staying in the prayer energy that has been created during the day.

A cottonwood tree, seen as a relative, serves as an altar, representing the tree of life. The tree serves as a conduit or vortex of great energy and is selected months before the dance. Each month, the community gathers around the tree and prays with the tree. The tree is seen as a brother and is respected. On the fourth day of purification, the entire camp gathers to do the ceremony with the cottonwood tree and cut it down for the Sun Dance ceremony. A young girl from the community is the first one to touch the ax to the tree, which represents the innocence of the child and the feminine virtues. The men then cut it down and carry it back to the ceremonial grounds. The tree becomes an altar for the dance and is placed in the center of the arbor, where the dance takes place.

The Native Americans believe that the most precious gift the Creator has given us in this physical world is the physical body. Women have the opportunity to give the blood of their body monthly and in childbirth. Because men weren't created to give birth, they choose to pierce their chests to give of their blood. The Sun Dance occurs during the fullness of the summer energy. The sun dancer dances prayers that give gratitude for life and that the people may live.

The dance is a time of revealing and healing of old ways of being, and it is used to set a heart intention that will go with one throughout the year. The ceremony humbles a person and brings him or her back to a sacred place of gratitude. There is a release of the heavy mental and emotional energies. There is also a focus and dedication to walking a good walk and being a spiritual warrior for peace.

From a place of prayer, men are pierced with a wooden or bone peg in their pectoral muscles. They choose what day and round of dance to pierce. At the end of a round of dance, the Sun Dancer dances back from the Sun Dance tree three times. On the fourth time, the pegs and the rope return to the tree as they pop free from flesh of the chest. Sun Dancers dance four days from the time the sun comes up in the east to the early evening when the sun is preparing to set in the west.

The Sun Dance is a warrior's dance, and only men originally participated. There are Sun Dance leaders who accept women to dance and pray. I asked High Star because he was in a position as a spiritual medicine man to grant a woman the right to dance. He shared that when a woman had a vision of sun dancing, he honored the vision. True visions come from the spiritual place within us all. The ego edges God out; a dancer would burn in the sun if the ego led the dance. Only a spiritual intention to pray in a good way brings blessings.

When I witnessed a Sun Dance ceremony for the first time, I knew my position was to pray for the dancers. I sincerely offered prayer day and night. I knew that they were dancing without water or food, and that each had a focused point of dedication to the celestial energy of Great Spirit. I was told by High Star that it was prayer that sustained the dancers.

When I observed the endurance and commitment of the dancers, I questioned whether I would ever be able to dance my prayers for hours in the hot sun. I asked dancers what sustained them and what fed them. I asked a strong lady dancer what assisted her in dancing, and she replied, "I become a blade of grass. The grass is wet with rain, and then the sun comes to dry the grass. The wind tries to flatten it, but the grass clings to its roots. I became a blade of grass, a Sun Dancer."

I knew something was calling me. The voice was constant and strong; I could hear it singing from the sun overhead. It was also coming from my feet, which didn't miss a beat of the drums. At the end of the last round of dancing, there was a request for those who had been called to dance next year. I stepped into the great arbor circle of dance to pledge to dance the next summer. With my skin white as the snow, I stood tall next to my brothers and sisters with their beautiful brown skin.

During the Sun Dancing, I surrender to the light of the sun and dance my prayers. The sound of the drums opens each flowering petal of my chakras within me, and I become one with it all. I release the fear into the moment and begin the prayer. It's easier to be in ceremony dancing my prayers than it is to walk the path of worldly demands and egoistic ways of perception that hold a person in the claws of fear. Sun Dancing has become my spiritual boot camp. Uncle Albert White Hat Sr. always reminded the dancers that the real Sun Dance began once the Dance was over: to walk the wisdom and to be the light of the sun.

I have become a blade of grass in my mind many times.

Life's Reflections

1. How do I dance my path of truth daily?

2. What is the meaning of dancing my prayers?

Prayer

To all that is and has ever been, I open my heart and stretch my arms to the heavens. I ask to feel the connection of earth and sky. Make a prayer through me! I release and let go, allowing the movement of the Creator to be experienced through each energy center of my being. I am grateful to dance until I become the dance.

Many Native American Indians have used fetishes throughout history, especially the Zuni tribe of Southwest Indians.

A fetish is an object which that is believed to have magic powers. Native Americans of the Zuni tribe believe if you place a small amount of corn meal under the nose of a Zuni bear image when you leave your home, the fetish will protect it while you're away. It is believed to have inhered powers or qualities that may aid the owner; its strength is therefore passed on to the owner. The meaning of the heart line symbol signified a life force.[22]

Chapter 14

LETTING GO TO THE GREATER

I want to Dance with You One More Time

The greater story of my transformation continues to unfold like the wild iris flowers in the night. For my first Sun dance, my clear intention was to dance and pray for the healing of my beloved daughter, who, in the spring prior to the summer Sun Dance, had been diagnosed with a brain tumor. This was shocking news for our entire family. At the time of the diagnoses, she was working as a hospice nurse, and she was in her final semester of

---

[22]   "Native American Symbols." Retrieved from http.//www.warpaths2peacepipes. com/native-american-symbols/zunibear.

graduate studies for a doctorate degree in nursing. I was a pastoral care minister at the time, and I had been attending to at least two people a month who had been diagnosed with brain tumors. I told my daughter, "There is nothing too big for God!" My intention to dance and to pray in this ancient way became stronger.

In meditation I realized a reoccurring family theme. My father received a severe head and brain injury in World War II. Then there were my own struggles with dyslexia as a child, and now my daughter had a brain condition. Even though my father had been physically deceased for years, could all of the family conditions be touched and healed by an unseen mysterious energy? The rest of this story reveals an amazing healing.

My intention to dance and pray in this way was for the healing of my daughter. My first vision quest with the big storm and the lightning offered to me the courage to ask permission from the elders of the dance and High Star to pierce my arms with small choke cherry sticks and to be connected by rope from each of my arms to the Sun Dance tree. I was shown in my vision to pray this way, and my daughter's challenge enforced my vision.

The early morning of the second day of my first Sun Dance was pleasant, and the sun slowly rose in the east as we entered the arbor to dance and pray in this sacred way. The pulse of drums and the songs of prayer lifted my feet as I danced.

The second round of dancing began, and the leaders danced me to the center to pray at the tree before being pieced. In the Lakota culture and tradition, the men precede the women. However, one of the leaders called me first, saying, "You are a minister, and is this your first time to pierce?" I nodded my head and knelt on a buffalo hide with my chin lifted to the sky. High Star pieced both of my arms and said, "Listen to the drums for it is the heartbeat of Tunkasila (Grandfather)." My arms felt a flash of burning pain, and the coolness I felt was my own blood running down my arms. I stood and thanked the dance leader.

After thanking the elders for the honor of dancing and being connected to the tree, my vision quest brother, Christian, was my supporter at the tree. He assisted me in dancing back from the tree. Christian was my Hanbleceya brother because he was also out in the storm and vision questing the night I'd danced with lighting. Everyone loved Christian for his generous heart and soul; I could not have asked for a greater supporter to assist me and dance by my side.

My rope was attached to the wooden pegs so the ropes pulled on my arms. Christian was dancing by my side. I began to pray, and every time my feet touched the earth with the rhythm of the drumbeat, my arms lifted to the sky. I leaned back and surrendered to the dance as the rope tightened. I could sense other sun dancers and supporters behind me who had entered the arbor to support me in my piercing experience.

I felt the moment when Christian stepped back from my side. I danced the second round of dance, and at the end of the second round of dance, I had the opportunity to break free from the tree. The ritual is to dance four times to the tree and back to one's place in the circle. During the fourth time dancing back from the tree, I prayed and danced like no one was watching. Then the rope and choke cherry stakes broke clean from my arms, and my flesh was given to the tree.

Immediately, clouds gathered, and wind began to swirl with great breath! Rain fell in buckets and instantly filled the arbor. My feet were like egg beaters in the mud and water. It wasn't the blood from the piercing running down my arms now but the rain washing me. The storm was strong, and my wet cotton dress was hit by the wind. I was dancing on several inches of water with the mystical grace of a deer; I leapt through the wet and muddy storm. Had I evoked a storm of this magnitude, or was this common during the Sun Dance?

The storm blew in sheets of rain and hail. This was an exceptional storm, and the leaders of the dance asked our supporters to go back to the camps to bring blankets for the dancers. Dancers were allowed a few moments to warm themselves near the sweat lodge fire. I saw strong men standing back to back and chest to chest to exchange heat and hearts. Out of the grayness of the storm, someone handed to me a green woolen army blanket. I appreciated the warmth of the blanket, and when the time came to set it down, I thanked the blanket like it had been an old, lost friend.

The female Sun Dancers had been asked to take refuge in one of the big tepees. Leaving the tepee to go back into the arbor to dance was like diving into a vast, freezing cold ocean. By the end of the day, my feet were webbed and waterlogged. The day was impactful from piecing, praying, and surrendering to the storm.

Back in camp after a long day of dancing in the storm., I asked who contributed the army blanket which had warmed and comforted me. No one seemed to know where it came from or who had brought it to me.

I mentioned my father had been severely wounded in World War II when he was an army scout in the high Italian mountains. When he was hit with fiery bullets from the enemy, his helmet crashed into his head. Two surgeries were performed in army tents on the mountain, and he had six more surgeries in Europe before coming back to the United States. Dad had constant head pain while I was growing up, and this was a challenge when I was a small child. Dad lived thirteen years after his injuries. His doctors called him the miracle man.

So many years after his death, I was dedicated to the highest and most sacred healing for my daughter's brain tumor. My intention was for her healing, and I never imagined my father was also released from the astral plane of pain and suffering.

Christian, who was honest and sensitive, approached me and asked permission to share the reason he had moved back from dancing by my side in the arbor earlier that day. "It wasn't because of the rain. Your father came and said to me, 'I just want to dance by her side one more time.'" It was amazing because Christian's description of my father was perfect, and he'd never seen a photo of him.

We sat in the aura of wisdom that evening, sharing this incredible story with High Star. We wanted to know who brought me the army blanket, and we shared Christian's experience. He said that my commitment and strong intention to pray and dance in a primal prayer ceremony like the Sun Dance had the capacity to open all dimensions of my life. He observed that soldiers (who had been conditioned to defend and kill) had many times experiencing their trauma, which lived on an astral plane.

The astral plane is an emotional and subjective band of energy that surrounds the earth long after the trauma or even after someone's physical death from this place of existence. High Star continued. "You gave your flesh and blood in a prayerful way in ceremony today, and therefore your whole family was healed this day! Your father's soul is free of the trauma of war. No one can find or knows about the army blanket that was offered to you in the arbor, so consider it your spirit blanket."

My daughter was home in Colorado, and when I arrived back home, she told me the day I had been pierced, she'd had a dream that night about my father, her grandfather, whom she'd never known. She was told to stop a certain medicine she had been prescribed and to trust her divine plan. Stopping the medicine proved to be beneficial for her well-being.

Since that day, I refer to my father as Papillion (butterfly) because he came to walk upon the water in the rain and is now free to dance. I was honored to dance with him one more time. I give thanks for the multiple levels of wholeness coming together in harmony and balance. We must remember life is not about the storms; it is about dancing in the rain.

Life's Reflections

1. How have the storms of my life brought spiritual healing and transformation?

2. Who dances by my side?

Prayer

This day, I accept the miracle and transformation of storm, prayer, undivided love, and the warmth of the Creator's heart. I celebrate the flight of the butterfly touching the water and rising in freedom. I am grateful for the glory of life.

Part Four

THE PATH OF TRANSFORMATION

Chapter 15

THE ROBE OF MY SOUL—MY BODY

"Life is a luminous halo, a semi-transparent envelope surrounding us from the beginning of consciousness to the end." —Virginia Woolf

 "I'm a cosmic bear. You will not find me featured in *Cosmopolitan* magazine. I have but one robe: it's my body. My body is sewn together with golden threads. I believe they are cosmic in nature."

What are the golden threads that hold life together? We have been cut from a cosmic tapestry of life. There is a love-intelligence that is natural. Its action is love, and its intelligence is the alchemy that is present upon this planet and in the planet's atmosphere. Each of us is a tapestry of the divine, a living organism. I perceive the human body as a bundle.

The golden threads, DNA, are the molecule of life. All organisms have their genetic material codified as DNA. In his book *The Cosmic Serpent DNA and the Origins of Knowledge*, Jeremy Narby shares, "The duplication mechanisms are the same for all living creatures. The only thing that changes from one species to another is the order of the (genes) letters."[23]

This constancy goes back to the very origins of life on earth. According to biologist Robert Pollack, "The planet's surface has changed many

---

[23]   J. P. Tarcher, *The Cosmic Serpent* (New York: Putnum Inc., 1998), 90.

times over, but DNA and the cellular machinery for its replication have remained constant. DNA is stability upon the planet."[24] According to Wikipedia, DNA consists of two long chains forming a double helix; this golden double helix thread is the code of creation. Our physical bodies are a sacred bundle of cosmic divinity. Carlton Pearson wrote, "We are limbs and ligaments of divine nature. Human beings are sharers in Divinity. We are germs of Divinity. Literally the genes of God. In other words, we possess the DNA of God."[25] It can be seen as the life and energy of the soul.

A bundle of flesh and bones is a bundle of love. "Love is the very fire and action of Infinite Spirit Itself."[26] DNA—divine natural assimilation. I know now what the saying "We are all related" means.

I believe life's code is love. Harmonic love is the glue that holds the stars in the sky and gives to each of us a species to identify with and a prototype.

Divine natural assimilation is golden in essence. The essence of humans, animals, and plants belong to a soul family. Every plant and animal species has a soul. Could the soul be the master cell? Could soul be that component of us that is pure DNA? Divine natural assimilation is a bridge of transmutation. In Bruce Lipton's book *Spontaneous Evolution*, he states,

> In the quantum Universe where everything is connected, love is the glue that holds things together. Laskow said, "Love is a universal pattern of resonant energy." In this sense, two or more tuning forks vibrating together are in love with each other, just as two or more humans can resonate in a palpable field of connectedness, joy, and even ecstasy Love. A lifetime without love is of no account. Love is the Water of Life. Drink it down with heart and soul.[26]

---

[24] R. Pollack, *The Cosmic Serpent* (New York: Putnum Inc., 1998), 674.

[25] C. Pearson, *Gospel of Inclusions: Religious Fundamentalism to the True Love of God and Self* (New York: Atria, 2009), 46.

[26] B. H. Lipton and S. Bhaerman, *Spontaneous Evolution* (California: Hay House, Inc., 2009), 287.

All goes back to love. Love is life: omnipresent, vital energy. The word *soul* stands for "Spirit; Omni, Unity, Living." Accept your union with Creation. Life is Love.

Life's Reflections

1. What is the cosmic glue?

2. What are ways I stay conscious to my divine connection?

Prayer

I recognize the God divine presence. The presence is found in and through all of life. I AM that I AM God divine. I realize, see, feel, and know the movement of divine natural assimilation manifested in my life and in all of life. My very breath is a conduit of divine connection. I am forever love; I am forever grateful.

Chapter 16

THE PHARMACY OF LIFE

 "I understand the plant world. I'm known as the great physician. I have always listened to the plants and known their properties. Walk upon the dry leaves until they turn into flower petals. The very roots of the plants are anchored in the crystal core of Grandmother."

It has been speculated by medicine people of the south that the Star Nations have given healing plants to our planet. Within the plants of the rainforest and upon the mountains is the wisdom to heal any illness. The plant world beholds great intelligence. Medicine people look for the signature symbol in the plant world that represents the human illness. There is divine natural assimilation (DNA) in all living things. Shamans of all cultures and Holy Sages such as Jesus were familiar with the multiple dimensions of spiritual awareness.

While visiting the Amazon jungle of Peru, I had the opportunity to experience the power and grace of the Mother of plants, Ayahuasca. The medicine was administered in a sacred way. My realization was one of brilliant colors, seeing the many dimensions. There was a harmony and joy which I had never known before. I had no expectations, and I was able to pierce through my veils of judgment and concerns to awaken within me that which never sleeps. There were no doubts that cosmic light shines brighter than white. I saw this outside of myself, but now I could see it within myself as well. My humanness, in the greatest moments of my life, had never known this. The medicine seemed to know exactly what I needed to know.

Throughout the night, the jungle's heart of trees and plants sounded the Eternal Om for me. Amidst the morning cloud forest was a new dawning, and as I walked upon the dew of the morning, the vines and plants smiled. It was the best of days! I never forgot what a wise old German woman had said to me years ago: "There is one life and many experiences of it."

Everything has a physical and celestial body. "If there is a physical body, there is also a spiritual body. The spiritual body is the first body and is the life force that whirled and wore the golden helix of divine natural assimilation. This spiritual body is always presence. It is the energy of love, and we can call it forth to fuse every physical cell of our bodies. Let us know that the energy of love is the original and only blessing. It is the DNA component that transmutes and beholds this powerful blessing as and into our lives.

Every series of life has a soul group, which is its pattern. For example, bears have a soul spirit group. All animals, plants, and humans do. When bears wander into the city, they become disorientated. As humans, we become disorientated when we stray from our divine patterns. We poison our bodies and our minds with substances that do not nurture us. We build an energetic current of dependency with false substances. The natural fibers of our physical body ask to be stimulated by natural fruits, grains, and appropriate amounts of food. The body asks to experience an inner cleansing with water daily. Taking care of our bodies is a daily spiritual practice.

Life's Reflections

1. What ways do I salute the divine pattern in all beings?

2. What are ways I nurture my body temple?

Prayer

The living spirit is present in and through all of life. I celebrate the divine current of Love-Intelligence that flows through me. I am the mineral, plant, tree, and life that lives within the sea. I'm a soulful expression of divine grace. I live forever within the multidimension of cosmic life. I am grateful!

Chapter 17

BEYOND THE DREAM

"Death is an experience of one's own intimacy." —Evan Hodkins[27]

 "What is transformation? I come from the energy of the West, which represents transformation. Can you shape-shift like I can? Transformation is to transfer into energy forms. Transformation is to alter form. When I die, I set down my body and recreate life."

In lucid dreaming, you are conscious and unconscious at the same time. Perhaps this is being aware of the particle and the wave at the same time. This realization has been referred to as the veil of unconsciousness. "There are many rooms within my Father's mansion. If this was not so, I would have told you. I go to prepare a place for you."[28] This quote from Master Jesus speaks of the different veils of consciousness. Moving through the different veils of consciousness requires the awakening and lighting of particles. Particles are form, and form is constantly changing. Our bodies are forms, and life around us is shaped into form.

There is an intimacy that brings forth the embrace of the deepest nature. True intimacy is the experience of "seeing into me," meaning the realizations of our divine nature. It the awareness of the unity where there is no sense of other. Intimacy is established in ways that reveal our wholeness. The particles of personality are set aside and the lights of our beings is seen; we are stripped of judgments and humbled in the light of truth. "We die before we die." We let ourselves out of the bottle of controlling confining selfish ways. Our conceptual mental minds have expanded too much for the bottle, and the bottle must be broken.

---

27   "Lecture Notes: Death as a Spiritual Teacher," Boulder Graduate School, Boulder, CO, 1990.

28   The New Oxford Annotated Bible, Revised Standard Version (Oxford University Press, 1971), 2032.

Many times our egos selfishly edge God out of our life equations. Our consciousnesses become larger than the egos that contained them. We see creation unfolding from consciousness and we are able to observe life.

The observer who moves from the broken bottle, from the particle to the wave, dances with reality. A perfect example of this is in birthing. Whether it is birthing a living soul into this plane of existence or the birthing called death into the next place of experience, both experiences are a rite of passage. Many have called this waking up beyond the dream.

If this is the case, why do we resist death? Is it because death is really all we know? Death is a change of form. Reverend Carl Scovel said, "So many little deaths we die before we die the big one. We die these deaths so we may live, so we may move with that inexorable force called life, The favorite mug smashed on the stone floor, the lost book, the job gone, the song sung, the face now seen only in that unrealistic photo-all these are part of the dying-to-live."[29] The forms of our thoughts and our physical forms are constantly changing. Like a reptile, we shed out of falsehoods of ego identifications. So why do we resist death? Could it be because we hold to the particle form as our identities and not the wave?

Death is instinctual to all species of all the creatures on the planet; it is the human who is emotionally attached to things and other humans. I believe humans resist because of the emotional buffering that surrounds the attachments. Emotional buffering seems to be attachments and expectations. In doing this, the human loses sight of his instinctual primary responses to letting go.

We forget that to physically die is to be birthed by detaching and releasing the physical. The physical represents the particle and birthing. We let go to become the wave. We lift the veil of unconsciousness to experience what is beyond the dream. Deepak Chopra stated,

---

[29]   C. Scovel, *Never Far From Home: Stories from the Radio Pulpit* (Boston: Skinner House Books, 2004).

This lifetime of ours is transient as autumn clouds. To watch the birth and death of beings is like looking at the movements of a dance. A lifetime is like a flash of lightening in the sky rushing by like a torrent down the steep mountain. But now I am free. I am grounded in being. I am grounded in the infinite consciousness and I can see lifetimes ripple by waves in the vast ocean of consciousness. I am free. I am awake. I am liberated.[30]

In childbirth, the mother can be fearful because it is a seemingly unknown experience. But what does the baby experience? Does it leave its place of intimacy to ride the wave into conscious awareness of its particle form? Is the wave represented by breath as we birth into the experience of death and leave the body, the form, behind? Either way, I believe it's a sacred moment of liberation.

I have been with several people who physically have been birthing into what we call death. There has been the experience of individuals being unconscious (coma) with only the sense of sound available to them. The five senses begin to dissolve during the death process. I believe the sense of sound is the vibratory frequency that rides the wave. Perhaps it is the soundless music of life that carries us. Is there an absence of movement in death? What appears as an absence is evident only in the physical. The point of change called death is the experience of one's own intimacy. We ride the golden ribbon of breath called the wave.[31]

Where does the breath go when we die? Many years ago, I was given the honor of attending to a beautiful woman who was in the transition of surrendering her physical body to the birthing process I call death. At the moment of her passing, I saw a spiral of pure white light moving from the crown of her head, circling the room like a helix ribbon of bright light. I accepted that it was the visible presence of spirit. Her soul was riding the wave of divine light!

---

[30] D. Chopra, *A Monk's Journey* (2012). Retrieved from https://www.deepakchopra.com/video/article/713.

[31] D. Chopra and A. Plack, *The Secret of Healing Meditations for Transformation and Higher Consciousness.* Retrieved from www.deezer.com/tl/album/975188.

As Ernest Holmes said, "We are bound because we are first free, and the power which binds us is the only thing in the universe which can free us. Man already has, with himself, the key to freedom but he must come to realize his relationship to the Whole."[32]

Life's Reflection

1. What are my perceptions of death?

2. How do I die before I die?

Prayer

I behold the very presence of life. I salute the eternal continuum of love manifesting within all kingdoms of the divine. I'm an eternal being. I live from the place of divine blessing, forever and forever.

---

[32]   E. Holmes, *Science of Mind* (Los Angles: Science of Mind Publishing, 1974).

Chapter 18

A THOUSAND SUNS

Winter

Bear Cycle

Fall   *Spring*

Hibernation (Death)   *Emergence from Den (Restoration)*

For what is it to die but to stand naked in the wind and to melt into the sun?" —Kahlil Gibran[33]

 "The sweetness of the moist grasses and the crystal clear smell of midnight ... What does midnight smell like? On a clear night, the air is as light as a feather. Sitting and gazing into the starry light, I close my eyes and become a part of it all—the moon and the patterns of diamonds of light."

The summer of 1998 was my second vision quest. My best friends, Sue and Jerry, were my vision quest supporters. Uncle Percy Bad Hand held the prayers for this event.

On my second vision quest, I experienced the power of direct sun and the power of my body beginning to melt in the sun. The sun is intense and dries up the rain; the plants open their faces to the sun in full humility, and their fragrance emits gratitude for the moment. The sacred elements of earth, air, fire, and water remind all of life to be humble to the power of the elements. It reminds us that we only walk on water when it rains.

---

33   K. Gibran, *The Prophet* (New York: Knopf Publication, 1980), 81.

I was placed on a hillside with no trees. I remember how sweet the night was. Upon hearing the strange sound of swirling ropes overhead, I knew that the spirit world was present with me. I chewed on the tall grass for its sweet water. The nighttime was peaceful, but the sun came up early. The humidity was like wet clay crowding out my breath. In front of me on the hillside, two large monarch butterflies flew back and forth, setting the stage for my transformation. I believe they were the warm-up act preceding the main performance.

I felt as though there were a thousand suns shining down upon me. I took the sage I was sitting on and began to weave a covering for my head. The sun sucked water from my body. My arms began to curl up like big plant leaves wilting in the sun. I prayed that my supporters would come for me. I was melting into the sun. I had been on the hill all night and all day in the direct sun.

Suddenly, Sue and Jerry's faces were right in front of me. There was an inner smile on my heart, and I wanted to speak but physically couldn't. Sue and Jerry were alarmed by my grayish, pale clay face. They carefully helped me walk up the hill and placed me in the truck. They insisted that I sip water.

Back at camp, I was immediately put into a sweat lodge. After prayers were spoken, I was placed outside to cool with the setting sun. I remember saying to the sun, "I almost went with you, never to be seen again." The sun winked at me and slipped beneath the horizon.

I know what it's like to stand naked in the wind and melt into the sun. The butterflies never left me, and their profound, subtle presence held the great story of transformation.

Life's Reflections

1. What has been my experience of death?

2. Have I felt the presence of the butterflies?

Prayer

Holy eternal life is everywhere present. My body is the robe of my soul, and my soulfulness lives forever within the cosmic light of Spirit. I am held within the cosmic cell, and I live forever free. I give thanks for the beauty and presence of the beautiful, which is the soul of my being. The butterfly knows how to shift graciously. I am grateful for my clay vessel of light.

Part Five

THE PATH OF COSMIC LIGHT

*"We awake to the religion of nature, which is the only religion.
And the more we understand it, the greater our life becomes,
and the more of a blessing will our life be for others."*

Khan

Chapter 19

Beams of Light

 "What is it to roar on a cool night and to connect with the stars overhead?"

The roar is the humming within me that emanates in nature. It's the inner drone synthesis of all sound. It's my song, and I sing with the birds and roar with the lions and other bears. Never forget your preciousness as a spiritual being. Your role is a big one: to lead the people to the waters of spiritual truth. Be not afraid of your voice. Remember to look for the tall people, for they have come from the stars, the heavens above you. They know your name, and the drone is a frequency and has nothing to do with language as you know it. You will hear it when you are totally still.

There's a dimension to the night, and it comes alive. Friends pass my path, and I greet them with a smile. I sit in the moonlight and wish upon a star.

At times, the mystical path consumed me like a burning coal on a winter night. The night, bright with a million stars, smiled at me. This was my fourth vision quest, and I had asked to be placed in the location where I'd first vision quested and danced with lightning.

One quest led to another, and now I consciously sat on Grandmother Earth's back and looked to the night sky, fully awake and aware. Immediately and mysteriously, a beam of light entered from the left of where I sat. It was a large bar of the whitest light I could imagine. It was a big beam of light, like a bar of light from a fiery steel furnace, brighter than bright, rising to the right of me. Was this a galactic experiment? I heard sounds like beeping cell phone chatter. There was an open window behind me, like the galactic broadcasting had set up their site. I was peaceful and not afraid. It was hard to say how long this experience lasts;

I was in a timeless space of mind. I listened to the celestial chatter, and as quickly as it appeared, it vanished.

When the mystical path opened to me, I was glad I didn't say, "Beam me up, Scotty!" or click my heels three times like Dorothy in *The Wizard of Oz*. I'd always known that I was in the spotlight of divine beings.

A double rainbow had appeared to me in the morning hours after my first vision quest. Now in the cool midst of night, the song, "Somewhere Over the Rainbow" went through my mind. The sky inside a primary rainbow was brighter than the sky outside of the bow. The raindrops that made up the brilliant rainbow reflect the light. The rainbow, bright in the colors of the spectrum, was calling me to acknowledge the drop of water, the raindrop, and to honor water, which is life itself. It was asking me to stretch my thinking to go beyond the rainbow and discern life. Was this galactic light? Was it discernment of my greater expression of life? What was behind the rainbow?

High Star shared the vision within in my experience upon the hill in my questing time. "The star people look at ancient ritual and observe it." I was told it was a divine appointment. It was my awareness of greater realization of cosmic life and light.

The stars shine brightly upon us, each one a sound of a tiny bell ringing forth stardust. Rest in the light, for the light shows you the way. The darkness will show you the stars.

"It's springtime now. Become the spring flowing, ever flowing. Trust the dance. In the circle of bear is the grandfather, grandmother, and all living creation. A little club, curious and bold, is rolling and stirring the dust. Sit in the circle of bear and bare your soul. Let your hands feel the earth and bask in the rays of eternal sunlight. We're one in this family of bears. We are one in this circle of bears."

Chapter 20

COSMIC CIRCLE OF LIFE

"The power of the world always works in circles and everything tries to be round. The sky is round, and I heard that the earth is like a ball, and so are all the stars. The wind in its greatest power whirls; birds make their nest in circles, for theirs is the same religion as ours. The sun and moon, both round, come forth and go down again in a circle. Even the seasons form great circles while they're changing, and always come back again to where they were. The life of a person is a circle from Childhood to childhood, and so it is in everything where power moves." — Lakota medicine man Black Elk[34]

"We all have an equal place on the circle of life that doesn't lessen or exalt others. Learn to listen with your feet and your hands. Open wide all of your senses, and know the sweet smell of midnight. We share the same cycle of life with other forms of life. The circle of stones is the earth herself. All of life is a circle and is illuminated to understand the circle."

Power moves outward. When a pebble is dropped into a shallow puddle of rainwater, the tiny ringlets push outward from the pebble, creating

---

[34]   J. G. Neihardt, *Black Elk Speaks* (New York: Kangaroo Books, 1977).

circles. The circle is a basic reality of life. The ringlet waves within a large body of water emanate outward. Energy does not emanate outwardly in any other shape.

All of life is a circle. Rainbows are circles even though we can only see half of the bright arched prism of light. The Inipi lodge, the tepee, the earth, the sun, and the moon are energetic circles. The sun and moon move in a circle. When a leaf jumps from a tree, it spirals in a circle and dances in a circle; it is propelled by the wind. The circle is the basic spiritual symbol representing life, and it becomes almost abstract as it runs into a cycle. There is the daily cycle from the darkness of night to the full sun of high noon and back to darkness.

What is circle intelligence? It is the divine pattern of our very own DNA as it spirals and produces living cells. Within a circle, there is no first and last, no higher or lower. All forms of life have a place on the circle. We are all born, and we all die within the life of the circle cycle.

The circle cycle contains darkness. Darkness is about a cycle, not about psychological shadows of emotional and mental upheavals. Light is in darkness, and darkness is in light. The opposite of love is fear, and fear is always self-concern. Breath is prana, universal energy. It is rhythmic, harmonious breathing that beholds spiritual light. "Rhythm pervades the universe. Everything from the greatest sun to the tiniest atom is in vibration, and has its own particular rate of vibration. The circling of the planets around the sun; the rise and fall of the sea; the breathing of the heart; the ebb and flow of the tide; all follow rhythmic laws. All growth and change is in evidence of this law."[35] Remember to breathe light into your day.

---

[35] Y. Ramacharaka, *The Science of Psychic Healing* (Chicago: The Yogi Publication Society, 1937), 72.

Life's Reflections

1. Today I have fun and count the many circles that appear to me.

2. More ways I can be conscious of my breath are:

Prayer

I am the circle within the circle. I am the divine movement of spirit. I proclaim the softness of the flow of all cycles of understanding, compassion, and inner peace. May I stand in the center of the circle and hear my name.

Chapter 21

THE SYMBOL OF MASCULINE AND FEMININE

One cool foggy night, I sat wrapped in the energy of prayer. The misty fog surrounded me like a beautiful Hocoka (circle) of feminine grace. The breath of Mother Earth was moist with her presence. Was I seeing the gray fog mute to a soft bluish hue, or was it my imagination? Was it the goddess dancing in the whirl of the fog? Was it my imagination that the ancient cultures contained a healthy balance of masculine and feminine energies? In the moment, I had a reverence for nature and its extreme balance of masculine and feminine energies. It's the Taoist version of yin and yang. I continue to learn from my Native American brothers and sisters the properties of feminine and masculine energy. Feminine energy is a receptive energy. Masculine is a directing forthright energy. The dualistic nature of the two energies gives life. I have learned from studying Taoism that nature expands and constricts resulting in a harmonious balance.

We're living in a time and space where we must relearn the inner ecology of feminine and masculine energies. The masculine ignorance has stripped, maimed, and killed many of the ancient wisdom cultures due to not understanding the feminine energies and the need for a harmonious natural balance between the masculine and feminine.

Masculine/Feminine Symbol

Life Reflections

1. How do I embrace my feminine energy?

2. What are ways I feel a balance of masculine and feminine energies of my being?

Prayer

I recognize the presence of a Mother Father God. I feel the essence of a Love-Intelligence of Mother Father God pulsating within my breath. I behold the grace and the majesty of the creative power of Love-Intelligence. My spiritual wings are outstretched in perfect balance. I soar and fly and catch the thermals of consciousness. With a grateful heart, I let go to the greater good of life.

Part Six

THE BEAR'S PATH TO EMPOWERMENT

Chapter 22

BEARLY, BEARLY I SAY UNTO YOU

Fresh bear scat was near by the little tepee. I trusted that the Great Bear Spirit had communicated to the physical bear how respectful I was of his or her mountain. I knew the bears were out of their hibernation time and wouldn't have been surprised to see one of them. In fact, the only time I saw a bear was one day when my husband, Luke, and I were with our two dogs. We were sitting at the top of the stream, where water bubbled from the depth of Grandmother Earth. I had my eyes closed, praying, when I heard Luke say that my most respected friend was approaching. My dog, Maggie, was sitting in a regal pose next to me, and the only sound she made was a muffled woof. Our other dog sat perfectly still. The small, still voice within me said, "Be not afraid. Stay still and tune in. Observe and witness the bear before you." My eyes opened wide, and I watched the bear cross the little stream.

How courageous and regal the bear was as it fearlessly stepped from the water and continued its path. The bear seemed to know that "Courage, rooted in anger, is unintelligent, whereas fearlessness, rooted in love is based on a sound mind and clarity of vision."[36] The bear, living its full potential, gently continued walking its path.

When we can shift from fear to a place of stillness and peace, life reflects a clarity of seeing—seeing as God sees, with peace, assurance, gratitude, and love.

---

[36] T. Hora, *Beyond the Dream* (New York: The Crossroad Publishing Company, 1996), 178.

Who Do They Say I Am?

In *Bear-ology*, Sylvia Dolson said, "In many aboriginal cultures, the bear was revered as a great healer because the bear knew the secrets of the plants. Often portrayed as the plant gatherer in many Native myths, the bear is seen as a mysterious herbalist gathering medicines straight from nature's pharmacy. Even the names of many North American wild plants, such as Bear's Tongue, Bear's Wort, Bear's Tail, Bear's Paw, Bear Clover, Bear's Ear, Bear's Breath, Bear Moss, Bear Corn, Bear b\Bane, and Bear Berry reflect the Bear's widespread association with medicine and healing hand in all cultures."[37]

For many, a bear's hibernation and spring reappearance, often with newborn cubs, is seen as a symbol of resurrection and renewal. In all cultures, the bear is seen as a powerful symbol of the wild. Bear medicine can teach you to go deep within so that you can make your choices and decisions from a position of power.

Life's Reflections

If bear has shown up in your life, ask yourself some important questions.

1. Is your judgment off?

2. How about those around you?

3. Are you not recognizing what is beneficial in your life?

4. Are you not seeing the core of deep good within all situations?

5. Are you being too critical of yourself or others?

6. Are you wearing rose-colored glasses?

---

[37] S. Dolson, *Bear-Ology* (Masonwille, CO: PixyJack Press, 2009), 92.

Prayer

Most respectful friend, I give thanks this day for the animal kingdom and for the minerals, plants, and trees; for fire, water, air, and clay. I walk with a greater spiritual awareness. I am grateful to be the wildflower resting in the sun.

Chapter 23

THE GRIZZLY BEAR'S GUIDE TO SELF-EMPOWERMENT

 I live from a core level for myself and my family; I stand upon an inner spiritual awareness that all my needs are met, Human's stand upon a box I call a "should" system of expectations and desires, and it becomes their empire. The psychological ego based "should" system becomes a boxed operational and a personal approach to having wants and needs met. Therefore, the construction of cities, and electing officials on the promise of wanting and needing to "should" all over each other.

As a living soul, we all need to remember to live an angerless life. Casting thoughts of being provided for assists me in trusting my natural instincts to discover and uncover what it is that I need. For example, under almost every fallen piece of wood, there are the most nutritional bits of delight. I'm led by the smell of fresh berries to abundant berry patches. Open your whole mind and body to listening, being anger less, and being free.

Let's get back to the box I called the "should" system. The box represents your individuality and separateness, your confinement, and for some your causation. The template is conformity masquerading as falsehoods, which are covered over by shadows of fear, but they are often marked as tranquility. There is a lot of pretending to be whole or simple. You are living in the box that had been paint with false concepts on the outside with what you think other people want to see. Many of you will fight if another person wants to get into your space or box. You have what you call squatter's rights, and you do not budge. Bears sublease stumps without lots of attachments.

Humans create boundaries even when they create a safe space for their families and respect other inhabitants. It is fear that keeps them in a state of separation from the Creator.

The grizzly bear gets a bad rap because he's extra large. At times he's placed in a position to defend himself from invaders and threats of harm from unconscious humans, which can be human error.

It's like you harness yourselves in a huge bear trap of blame and self-condemnation. You might ask, "Does a bear shit in the woods?" The answer is yes. But ask a bear if they "should" in the woods, and the answer is absolutely not. People are the only creatures who anchor their reality in "should" thinking.

There is omni-active love-intelligence. Practice the presence and give thanks for the little things on your path, and all your needs will be abundantly met. The inner kingdom ushers in the outer because the inner realities have been realized.

Do bears always tell the truth, or do they hide things from others?

You know the answer is no, because only humans lie and cheat and steal from others. If a bear was physically sick, he'd be grubby and rambling through the woods with no focus. Perhaps I'd want to eat my friends if I was running a fever. Humans run a psychological fever and project their unconscious thinking about themselves on others. This projection of unconscious thinking fosters a sense of separation from the total realization of our spiritual wholeness.

What do you do when one of your bears is disarranged and has been wounded?

We take the "bearberry" and sit respectfully in prayer for the bear to heal. We trust the bear knows how to heal itself. Remember how the humans have watched what the bears eats when feeling physically ill. The bear honors the spiritual quality of resting for bear rests rejuvenate the body. Being tuned to our organic nature gives to us heath and joy.

I know we bears can be tempted to break out of our organic patterns. When we are tempted to enter into the human world we are in danger. When we as bear are being tempted and wonder from our organic patterns, mankind tags us. We are disorientated and receive three tags. After three tags we are shot. You humans tag or mark each other with your judgments. Humans shoot each other with projections when they find each other wrong. Projections are our unconscious thoughts of judgment of self that are tagged upon one another. Projections are like acid rain: they are both poisonous and toxic.

Equilibrium needs to be established within every aspect of life, which includes animals and the water within the human body. Fire brings equilibrium, and spirit sparks and rekindles in all. Remember who you are. Get out of your box and see, feel and sense your fire. Like a powerful sacred waterfall, you are the force. You are the power of water, fire, heart and breath.

I continue to be amazed at the ignorance of human beings and how they self-confirm themselves as separate beings.

Life's Reflection

1. What do I need to delete, in order to save what is really real to me?

2. How can my life be fuss-less?

Prayer

Make me an instrument of thy love and peace. I behold there is no interaction anywhere, only omni-action everywhere. I am an awakened spiritual being. I am anger-less, fuss-less, and free. Freedom comes to me through the light of love. I am grateful!

Chapter 24

PAWS OR CLAWS

 "Your hands, the original Palm Pilot, are instruments of the divine. They knock at the door, and door is opened. They have felt the body of Grandmother Earth when they toiled in the garden. Your hands are folded in prayer or shake another's hand; they've learned how to wave good-bye. Your hands have hurt and bled. Another hand has struck someone else in violence and caused harm."

Some people have claws, and people need to learn how to have pause. (paws). They need to learn how to extend their hearts through their hands in a warm, hearty handshake with another. Your Native American friends don't have to control anyone with a handshake; they shake with a gentle, warm hand.

My claws were given to me by the Creator to harvest roots from the earth. They are my own set of utensils, and I grasp and safely climb a tree because of them. When I was threatened by man, my claws tore flesh.

For humans, your claws became words and attitudes from a judgmental thought. You take your stand, defending your personal selves. Your fear comes from disconnection from the wholeness of life, your wild nature. You've forgotten your inner senses, which are the compass that guides and directs the flow of introspection. Fear causes your hair to rise up upon the back of your neck. Tune your whole being with song, stroke your hair, and calm yourself. You are not alone. Open within; open the doors to the greater web of connection. The animal kingdom knew of the great web of connection long before humanity. Don't forget to pause (paws) on your path.

Life's Reflections

1. Have I hurt another with my claws?

2. What are ways I can paws (pause) upon my path and smell the flowers?

Prayer

Moment by moment, I am attentive to the goodness of life. Each step is a blessing, and new vistas give me insights. I walk on the water when it rains. I embrace the warm sun and bathe in the full moonlight. I accept that I am a purple meadow flower, stretching my petals to the sun. I am grateful!

Chapter 25

THE BEAR ATTITUDES

Listen to your feet and turn to the sky. Why? Because you are a cosmic being.

- Tread lightly upon your path, and always keep your eye upon the trail.
- Know that you are bigger and wiser, and that your challenge is to not go to sleep.
- When you observe the field around you, stand tall; be a transcendent observer.
- Trust your dream time; sing to the moon. Awaken within your dream world, for you have never slept.
- Only work for berries. The source is infinite, and the supply is eternal.
- Stand in the fullness of sun. Look for the sun beyond the sun.
- Dance with Grandmother Earth until she enters your body.
- Sit daily in the golden field of essence and become the light.

 "I will let you go fly and I will see you in the starry moon. I live forever within your heart. I will find you in your dreams; know I'm a friend, a faithful guardian, just call my name and I will be there." —

"Come theologians, scholars, saints and sages, we're coming home. Life has a way of humbling you to walk above the line of firmament and not be better than another, but to be above the judgments and projections of the human condition. Now is the time to embrace a cosmic light. We only walk on water when it rains."

- Patty Luckenbach

"I must go now into the forest for a thousand winds call to me. The earth holds my body in the moon light."

Conclusion

ENTER THE FOREST
OF YOUR HEART

 "Seek and you shall find. Look up and discern the kingdom above and the kingdom below. Reach for the kingdom within and extend your energy. Claim yourself as the matrix of the divine. The tree of life will call to you. Seek softly and rise tall to climb and rest on a branch in the high noon sun."

Jesus stated, "The kingdom of God is in the midst of you."[38] It's the birthright of all beings, and this universal truth shines within all kingdoms: plants, animals, the ethereal kingdom of the air in which the winged ones fly, the life within the belly of Mother Earth, and the great sea and oceans. May we see with a sage's eyes. The holy people and extraordinary human beings perceive a harmonious connection—the cosmic patterns of the great life. "There is a language beyond the intellect and it is the language of the soul, whether it is singing or dancing or writing, painting, sculpting, or praying. Every man's life is a prayer to the God he believes in, and the God he believes in answers every man at the level of his or her belief."[39] There are no two blades of grass alike, no two people's fingerprints alike. Life seeks balance, a spiritual equilibrium in all life forms. How do we as humans realize our core equilibrium? Sages have referred to our cores as souls and spirits, saying it is golden in color. Some in the esoteric teachings have called it the master cell of our divinity. There is an organic, cosmic pattern for everything that exists in physical form. Perhaps when I state we have been stitched by an organic golden thread, there is greater truth than I have realized.

---

38   The New Oxford Annotated Bible, Revised Standard Version (New York: Oxford University Press, 1971).

39   E. Holmes, *The Anatomy of Healing Prayer*, compiled by George P. Bendall (California: Devorss Publications, 1991), 73.

Such spiritual giants as Ernest Holmes and countless others have looked for the golden thread that they felt was in all religions.

"I propose the question: Does God even care about religion? Life knows no one religion but knows only light. Let your light so shine so all beings may see it. You, as a spiritual being, are having a human experience. Seek to walk a harmonious, light-filled pathway. I notice how you designate and discern what the right path is. Religions seem to be attached to being on the right path."

Many years ago, I was asked by my pastor from my teenage years to represent my current ancient wisdom faith at an interfaith gathering at a retirement facility he was serving. My inner child looked forward to it because I knew they'd have homemade refreshment, but I didn't know whether the people at the gathering would find my spiritual principles and beliefs acceptable. I presented my program, and my former pastor immediately swept me away to his office. I wondered if it was something I had said.

He closed the door and said, "Patty, I've been a pastor for many years. There were times when I didn't have the answers. There have been times I felt hollow inside as a pastor. If I had to do it over again, I'd profess your spiritual beliefs. Your statement today—'The cosmic light, the one mind, one heart, the spirit beaming in each individual as the cosmic Christ light—is what I believe. The Christ light being present is a universal principle!" We both agreed that the living truth in the very action of God was love manifested in every human heart and soul. We together blessed all walks of faith, knowing the path of love is the path of heart. No one needs to be saved, but we do have the need to awaken to the spiritual truth. The life of God is my life now, and the kingdom is within all beings.

It was worth missing the cookies and punch, because we both were fed with sweet spiritual truth.

Spiritual equilibrium goes beyond religions and their support of a greater concept of a natural deity. The Native American believe "No one owned the Creator but shared in its life and essence."[40] Spirituality relates to the spirit or soul. Spirituality supports religious meanings in a sacred interchangeable way, always seeking spiritual equilibrium. Perhaps it's time to walk outside and look through our soulful eyes to the interconnection of all life.

Great minds have stated that there's a God beyond the rational mind of humanity. The cosmic matrix is beyond a human concept of God. It's the sun behind the sun, the God beyond God. Its sacred meaning is found in and through all people and all of life. It's beyond the sun, and it is an inner, humbling spiritual presence.

Life's Reflections

1. What were your childhood beliefs regarding religion?

2. Have your childhood beliefs changed?

Prayer

I behold the sacred presence of a living God in and through all beings. I bless all walks of faith. I affirm the greater light of love is revealed through every soul. I am grateful to know that the kingdom of every lasting life is a divine presence radiating the vibrating light of love.

---

[40]   C. A. Eastman, *The Soul of the Indian* (Acorn Publishing, 1911).

THE PATH OF FEATHERS

The path of feathers has given to me the prayerful experience of sinew pieced through the skin of my arms, holding the eagle feather to my body as I dance and fly. I dance my prayer for the awakened consciousness of all beings, for all people to come together in sacred love. I pray for all humanity to awake in consciousness. I sing with my grandchildren. The path winds its way upward, and I continue to dance and pray, sing, and watch the butterflies whirl. Life is eternal. The involvement of the flowing cactus in the night light of the desert has revealed miracles and mystical messages.

The eagles soar overhead, and I celebrate the connections of heaven and earth. The eagle feather whirls and spins in the wind, which humbles me with the courage and faith to keep dancing. The pathway of feathers represents to me an awareness of the connection of earth and sky.

The many native teachings explain that eagle is the principle messenger of the Creator. Eagle flies the closest to the Creator, and therefore he can see the past, present, and future at a glance. Eagle is connected both to the spirit of Great Mystery and to the earth.

From this connection of earth and sky, I was told after my first vision quest that I would take the prayer pipe to the south. Two years ago, while surrounded by the great medicine of the plants, I shared with the medicine people of the jungle the prayers from the north. Honoring the masculine energy of the eagle feather and the great feminine energy of the powerful condor feather, we celebrated the union of the masculine and feminine coming together for the awakening consciousness of humanity.

Thich Nhat Hanh beautifully stated, "The miracle is not to walk on water. The miracle is to walk on the green earth, dwelling deeply in the present moment and feeling truly alive."[41] A Lakota teen proudly wore a T-shirt that read, "Life is not about the storms of life but how we dance in the rain." Humbly we walk and dance life's path of heart. The dance of life is not about dancing for others, but dancing within the core of our being. As we dance, our humility lets us rise above thought to the place beyond the dream. Every facet of who we are is of the whole, and it's the birthright of all nations. I salute the cosmic field, for it is from there that we dream and walk. I give thanks for the sacredness of rain. I am grateful to have been washed and cleansed. I am the Woman Who Dances with Lightning. I am most grateful.

---

[41] H. Halman, "Green Man: Seven Pillars House of Wisdom" (2015), retrieved from http://www.sevenpillarshouse.org/article/the_green_man.

BIBLIOGRAPHY

Barks, C., Green, M. *The Illuminated Rumi. New York*: Penguin Random House, Inc., 1997.

Chodron, P. *The Places That Scare You: A Guide to Fearlessness in Difficult Times*. Boston: Shambhola Publications, 2001.

Chopra, D. "A Monk's Journey." 2012. Retrieved from https://www.deepakchopra.com/video/article/713.

Chopra, D. & Plack, A. "The Secret of Healing Meditations for Transformation and Higher Consciousness." 2011. Retrieved from www.deezer.com/tl/album/975188.

Cowan, T. *A Pocket Guide to Shamanism*. Trevose, PA: Crossing Press, 1997.

Deloria, Jr., V. *Vision Quest*. New York: Crown Publisher, Inc., 2006.

Dolson, S. *Bear-Ology*. Masonville, CO: PixyJack Press, 2009.

Eastman, C. A. *The Soul of the Indian*. Beckenham, United Kingdom: Acorn Publishing, 1911.

Gallegos, E. S. *Animals of the Four Windows*. New Mexico: Moon Bear Press, 1991.

Gilbert, E. *Eat, Pray, Love*. New York: Viking, 2006.

Gibran, K. *The Prophet*. New York: Knopf Publication, 1980.

Halman, H. "Green Man: Seven Pillars House of Wisdom." Retrieved from http://www.sevenpillarshouse.org/article/the_green_man.

Holmes, E. *The Anatomy of Healing Prayer*. compiled by George P. Bendall. California: Devorss Publications, 1991.

Holmes, E. *Light*. Los Angeles: Science of Mind Publications, 1980.

Holmes, E. *Science of Mind*. New York: G. P. Putnam's Sons, 1966.

Hora, T. *Beyond the Dream*. New York: The Crossroad Publishing Company, 1996.

Hora, T. *Compassion Booklet*. Orange, California: PAGL Press, 1985.

Howard P. "Bad Hand." Taoism workshop, Denver, 2011.

Kassen, S. *Rise up and Salute the Sun*. Boston: Awakened Press, 2010.

Lipton, B. H., Bhaerman, S. *Spontaneous Evolution*. California: Hay House, Inc., 2009.

"Lecture Notes: Death as a Spiritual Teacher." Boulder Graduate School, Boulder, Colorado, 1990.

Luther, M. *Christmas Book*. R. Bainton, ed. Minneapolis: Augsburg, 1948.

Miiguich, C. *Memories, Dreams, Reflection*. New York: Vintage Books, 1989.

Myss, C. *Entering the Castle*. New York: Free Press, 2007.

"Native American Symbols." Retrieved from http.//www. warpaths2peacepipes.com/native-american-symbols/zunibear.

Neihardt, J. G. *Black Elk Speaks*. New York: Kangaroo Books, 1977.

Nepo, M. *The Book of Awakening*. Newburyport, MA: Conair Press, 2011.

Pearson, C. *Gospel of Inclusions: Religious Fundamentalism to the True Love of God and Self*. New York: Atria, 2009.

Ramacharaka, Y. *The Science of Psychic Healing*. Chicago: The Yogi Publication Society, 1937.

Rosebud Quilts and Quilters. St. Francis, SD: St. Francis Mission.

Scovel, C. *Never far from Home: Stories from the Radio Pulpit*. Boston: Skinner House Books, 2004.

Smith, H.A. *Seattle Sunday Star*, October 1887.

Tarcher, J. P. *The Cosmic Serpent*. New York: Putnum Inc., 1998.

The New Oxford Annotated Bible, Revised Standard Version. New York: Oxford University Press, 1971.

White, G. "Written at the Rain Forest Benefit, NYC." Retrieved from www.whitelotus.org/articles/poem.html.

Images

Nelson, C. *Bear Face*. 2015.

Nelson, C. *Small Bear Paw*. 2015.

Nelson, C. *Large Bear Paw*. 2015.

Nelson, C. *Bear Reflection*. 2015.

Nelson, C. *Bear Looking over Its Shoulder*. 2015.

Luckenbach. P. *Feather*. 2015.

Luckenbach. P. *Circle of Life*. 2015.

Luckenbach. P. *Hibernation Cycle*. 2015.

Luckenbach. P. *Masculine/Feminine*. 2015.

Mile Hi Graphics. *Banner.*

Mile Hi Graphics. *Power Bear.*

Rosebud Quilts and Quilters. *Star Quilt.*

ABOUT THE AUTHOR

Dr. Patty Luckenbach is a well-known speaker, a profound and wise teacher, and the author of *The Land of Tears Is a Secret Place* and *The Kingdom of Heart*. For over twenty-six years, she has specialized in the care and nurturing of the human spirit as one experiences deep grief and loss from the constant changes in life. Dr. Patty is an associate minister of Mile Hi Church, Lakewood, Colorado, and is the director of the prayer and care center.

A Colorado native, Luckenbach received her master's degree in transpersonal psychology from Boulder Graduate School, and she holds an honorary doctorate of divinity from the Centers of Spiritual Living. Dr. Patty is a teacher and psychotherapist specializing in grief support services, psycho-spiritual growth, and journal writing as a therapeutic adjunct. Her greatest joy comes from facilitating others in stepping through the portals of life's changes. She lives in the Rocky Mountains with her husband, Luke, and her dog, Maggie Rose.

Patty Luckenbach has been gifted with being a part of the Lakota Sioux community. As a Sun Dancer for many years, she displays and lives from the place of a shaman's soul. "All of life is a sacred ritual of remembering our holy oneness with all of life."

Patty is a guide for questing for unity in the wilderness of consciousness. *I Only Walk on Water* is a sharing from her heart.